# Bilingu
# romance novel
# to learn French
# for beginners

*la beauté des changements*

Lucy Lagarde

1st edition
2025

"Learning a language means
having another window,
from which to view the world."

(Chinese saying)

# Dedication

**For Max**

Thank you
for making two windows
accessible to me.

I am very happy
to have you in my life
exploring intercultural differences
as well as funny misunderstandings
with you.

# Table of contents

# Preface

Dear reader,

Have you ever wondered what it would be like to experience a story exactly as it would happen linguistically in reality? This was exactly the idea at the beginning of this book - and it could change your language learning forever.

**The genesis**

During the Covid-19 pandemic, travelling was suddenly no longer possible, but my longing for international conversations remained. I love getting to know different perspectives and finding out how people in other cultures think - sometimes surprisingly similar, sometimes completely different. I am particularly fascinated by the topic of 'romantic relationships', as there are so many different views on the subject around the world.

In April 2020, I asked myself a question: what if I told an international love story - exactly as it would happen linguistically in reality? What started out as a creative project quickly developed into an exciting approach to language learning. Motivated by my growing interest in linguistic theories and encouraging feedback from a lexicographer, I refined the concept further - with the aim of creating an entertaining yet effective way to learn intuitively.

## The concept

This bilingual novel combines entertainment with proven language learning methods and is aimed at learners at A2 level. Here are some key principles that will help you to improve your foreign language skills in the long term:

Learning through emotions: Language is better remembered when it is associated with enjoyment, curiosity and interest. Studies show that adults often learn rationally, while children absorb language holistically. This book takes you back to playful, emotional language acquisition.

Storytelling approach: Stories are one of the most effective tools for learning. They arouse emotions, encourage associations and make it easier to remember new concepts.

Code-switching: In multilingual conversations, we often unconsciously switch between languages. This book makes targeted use of this effect to ensure realism and comprehensibility.

The OPOL approach (One Person, One Language): Similar to bilingual education, English characters speak exclusively in English, while foreign-language characters speak exclusively in their own language. This keeps the language separation clear and consistent.

Vocabulary help on the spot: Difficult terms are explained directly on the respective page in the footer so as not to interrupt the flow of reading. You will find a complete vocabulary list at the end of the book for repetition.

Space for notes: The generous formatting invites you to actively use the book - simply make a note of new words or thoughts in the margin.

Increasing level of difficulty: The proportion of foreign language gradually increases so that you can gradually get used to more complex structures.

Challenge and support: Although the vocabulary is geared towards A2 level, the book also contains more challenging grammatical structures - just like in real life, where we don't know every word but still understand the meaning.

## Your benefit

Every learning process is individual, but I know from previous feedback that readers have experienced the following benefits in particular:

- More fun with the foreign language
- Vocabulary learning as if travelling
- Refreshing and consolidating knowledge already learnt
- A sense of achievement in language learning
- More motivation and language confidence
- Realistic practice in authentic situations

**Your opinion counts!**

You have now gained an insight into how much heart and soul has gone into this project. That's why your feedback means so much to me! If you liked the book, I would be delighted if you would leave a review on Amazon - it not only helps me, but also other learners. Or write to me directly via the contact form on my website: www.bilingual-novels.com.

(An important note: unfortunately I can't reply directly to Amazon reviews, but I read every single one and take them very much to heart).

Now I wish you much joy and success with this bilingual story!

Best regards
Your Lucy Lagarde

# Chapter 1

"Surprise!"

I jump back in shock and try to calm my pounding heart. My parents' small living room doesn't look like it usually does. Around twenty people are huddled in there, laughing at me. From a sea of faces and balloons, I hear,

"Goodbye, Lily."

I see Kate, who is grinning particularly broadly. Of course, she is responsible for this farewell party. She's my best friend from my childhood and never lets me get away with anything. She jumps out at me and hands me a glass of champagne.

"To celebrate your last day," she says.

"I'd think you were *happy to* get rid of me," I reply with a grin and look around.

Just about all my friends are here. Even my parents are standing in the crowd, smiling shyly. They've been really great these past few weeks. I'm going to miss them.

"Nonsense, I'll miss you! But I'm happy about your next chapter in life and that you are being so brave!" Kate says.

I don't respond and stifle an "I *must be* brave!". My application to *Celuxe* in Paris has less to do with my courage and more with my consumption of sugar and vodka. These became my comfort after the break-up with Andrew. 'Breakup' might not exactly be the right word, either. A nasty ass piece of action describes it better. He cheated on me after a five-year relationship with his 'good friend'. As a result, I moved out of our shared flat to my parents. I made some bold decisions for the rest of my life during those nights I had with vodka, cake, and the internet.

Then the HR manager of Paris's hottest company called me. They like my style - I'm a graphic designer - and they'd like me to join the team. What was I supposed to do? At my current company, everyone knows about Andrew and me. We met there years ago, kept our relationship secret at first, and then gradually announced it. It worked well until we broke up, and something changed. But most of all, the strangest thing was how this change affected the connection between my boss and me. First, he kept gently asking me if I was okay. Later, in regular staff meetings, he told me that he felt my work performance was suffering because of my private 'circumstances'. At the same time, I was working as hard as I could and performing as before. I felt powerless and at his mercy. I had to change something. So, I was brave enough to finally accept the position at Celuxe, organise a flat share via a flat platform, and book a flight. And now there's no turning back.

It was a beautiful evening. My parents said goodbye and went upstairs around midnight— they will take me to the airport tomorrow morning—and my friends went home one by one, but not without a long hug and their best wishes.

In the end, only Kate and I remain. Tired, we lie opposite each other on the couch: my legs somehow become tangled with hers.

"I don't *really* want to leave..." I say and hiccup.

"What do you want?" asks Kate.

"I don't know. I'm nervous. I'm afraid I won't make it with the new job in Paris."

I throw a blanket over my head to emphasise the point. In the last few weeks, I've been going through many emotions, from anger about Andrew cheating to pure despair at my job to hope for a better time. I've even gained a few

12

kilos; sometimes, I don't even recognise myself in my emotional chaos.

"Nonsense," Kate says, laughing and pulling the blanket away from me.

"Of course, you can do it. You're the best graphic designer I know!"

"After all, I'm the only graphic designer you know," I tease her amusedly, nudging her amicably with my elbow.

"That's right..." she confirms thoughtfully and laughs to herself.

"But you'll see: Someday, you'll kiss Andrew's feet for cheating on you. This is your chance!"

And with these words - and a quietly growing doubt in my heart - I fall asleep.

# Chapter 2

I'm rushing through the airport. Everything went wrong this morning. I couldn't find my favourite jumper, so I couldn't finish packing in time. Then we were stuck in traffic for ages, and now the gate is at the other end of the airport.

"Excusez-moi, c'est bien le vol pour Paris?" I ask a steward, entirely out of breath. He points wordlessly with a raised eyebrow to a screen above my head, which clearly reads: Paris. I board the plane, fasten my seat belt, and can hardly believe it when the plane takes off.

"Des vacances en France?" the old lady with kind eyes in the seat next to me asks me when we are in the air.

I shake my head.

"Je commence une nouvelle vie," I say softly.

"Ah... C'est à propos de l'amour?" she asks.

I laugh with a snort. Of course, she doesn't mean any harm; just the thought that it's about love makes the corners of my mouth twist cynically.

"Non, je commence un nouveau **travail**[1] dans une **entreprise**[2] qui s'appelle Celuxe," I reply, "Je suis **graphiste**[3]."

"Ah, c'est merveilleux! Ma petite-fille n'arrête pas de me dire à quel point il est difficile de **trouver**[4] une bonne graphiste!"

The lady digs out a business card of her granddaughter and slips it to me. I think I'll have enough work for now, but I don't want to be rude, so I pocket it and listen to her talk about her

---

[1] travail – job, workplace
[2] entreprise – company, business
[3] graphiste – graphic designer
[4] trouver – to find

granddaughter's problems throughout the flight. As if I didn't have enough of my own.

And then suddenly I'm in Paris. I'm all alone for the first time in ages - and in a foreign city. I breathe in and out deeply. It's quite frightening. I miss my best friend, Kate, my parents and even Andrew for a small moment. I take a taxi, give the address and go wide-eyed as the taxi driver takes me through the city to my new flat. Paris is beautiful!

"C'est **tellement**[5] **beau**[6] ici!" I shout excitedly.

"Oui, maintenant, au **printemps**[7], Paris **se montre sous son meilleur jour**[8]," the taxi driver replies in a bored tone and pops a bubble of chewing gum.

---

[5] tellement – really, truly

[6] beau – beautiful

[7] printemps – spring

[8] se montre sous son meilleur jour – to show oneself from one's best side

I look at the houses, the colourful little shops, and the people sitting in the sun on the river banks. Finally, I arrived, and I rang the bell, even though the landlord sent me a key to England a week ago. I don't know the two women living here, and I would find it rude to walk in. But when no one opens the door for me, I finally unlock it.

"Bonjour? Il y a quelqu'un?" I called out carefully and pulled my suitcase behind me, which sounded incredibly loud in the silence of the flat. The flat is simple but pretty. I find the kitchen and decide to wait there for my flatmates.

When I open the fridge to get something to drink, all kinds of food fall towards me and tumble through my hands onto the floor. I sort out the mess, make myself a cup of coffee, and sit down at the table. But I can't stay seated for long because I'm so nervous, and I start cleaning the dirty tabletop.

Just at that moment, a young woman enters the kitchen. She has long reddish-blonde hair and bright blue eyes. She cries out in fright when she sees me crouching behind the table with a dirty rag in my hand.

"Qui es-tu? Et pourquoi tu **nettoies**[9] ma cuisine?"

Embarrassed, I drop the rag.

"Je m'appelle Lily. Salut!"

Her big blue eyes widen, and you can see her pause for a moment and think of something.

"Oh, bien sûr - tu es notre nouvelle **colocataire**[10]. **Au fait**[11], je m'appelle Poppy. Bienvenue!"

---

[9] nettoyer – to clean
[10] colocataire – flatmate
[11] au fait – by the way, actually

Amused, I stare at her. Suddenly, another young woman pokes her head into the kitchen. She has short, dark hair and a round, pretty face with which she looks around attentively.

"Qu'est-ce qu'il se passe ici... ?"

She spots me, gives me a big smile, walks towards me, and embraces me.

"Tu dois être Lily, non? Nous ne t'attendions pas si tôt. **Quoique**[12]... oups, il est déjà 17 heures. Je viens juste de **me lever**[13]."

She hands me a glass of wine without asking and talks in fast French with an interesting accent.

"Poppy et moi vivons ici depuis trois ans, **en alternant**[14] les colocataires. Paris est une ville

---

[12] quoique – although
[13] se lever – to get up
[14] en alternant – alternately

très internationale. Les gens viennent et s'en vont. Poppy est actrice et moi je travaille dans une petite **pâtisserie**[15]. Mais j'ai l'intention de me mettre à mon compte."

"Claire, laisse-la arriver," Poppy says and grins at me.

She has something tomboyish and mischievous about her, while Claire looks at me with an almost motherly smile. I like them both immediately. We spend the rest of the evening in the kitchen, where they tell me everything they think I need to know about the city. I haven't even unpacked yet, and I already know exactly where to get the best Ratatouille and where to go if I want to go dancing on a Monday night.

At the end of the evening, my head is buzzing, but as I lie in my new room, which for some

---

[15] pâtisserie – bakery, pastry shop

reason is full of posters of French 90s boy bands, I have a smile on my face.

I still have two weeks until my new job starts, and in the next few days, I will get to know Poppy and Claire. They have lots of suggestions, and they don't take no for an answer.

"Il faut que tu viennes dans ce bar. Il **ressemble**[16] à une jungle!"
"Ce café est **indispensable**[17]!"
"Nous irons danser plus tard. Tu viens avec nous, non?"
"Tu ne sais pas **à quel point**[18] les sushis peuvent être bons si tu n'es encore jamais allée chez Lu's!"

I haven't been on the go so much for years. It's unusual but cool and distracts me: I hardly think about home and even less about Andrew. I

---

[16] ressembler à qn.– to resemble someone

[17] indispensable – essential

[18] à quel point – how much

noticed that I had been hidden away in my relationship for the last few years. How could this have happened to me? I don't even know how to meet new people anymore. Let alone how to talk to men! I'm all out of practice when it comes to flirting. Not that I necessarily want to speak to men. But this new life here in Paris offers me many opportunities I haven't thought of in a long time. I feel like I am crazy and trying a lot of new things. I mean, what is the worst that can happen to me? I'm here to have new experiences, aren't I?

So, I get to know a lot of people pretty quickly. Poppy and Claire know exciting people from all kinds of countries and take me to all sorts of events. Poppy's circle of friends is full of crazy theatre people and artists, while Claire's friends praise good food, music, and dancing. The mix is always interesting. And in the middle of it all: Me - incredibly grateful!

One evening, when we are in the bar, which looks like a jungle with similar temperatures, I sit next to Louis, an attractive, tall Frenchman with whom I have not talked before. A palm tree grows out of the wall between us, and we have to keep pushing its leaves aside to talk to each other.

"Alors, ça te plaît ici à Paris?" he asks me. The music is loud, and we both must speak in raised voices.

"C'est pas mal **jusqu'à présent**[19]. Mais **à part**[20] les bars, je n'ai pas encore vu grand-chose," I reply, smiling through the leaves and sipping my wine. That's right. I know half the places in my district but haven't done any sightseeing.

"Si tu veux, je peux te montrer autre chose..." he says and grins.

---

[19] jusqu'à présent – up until now
[20] à part – apart from

"Désolé, je n'aime pas les hommes **bruns**[21]." I try to talk myself out of it and shrug my shoulders innocently. Although he doesn't look so bad, his light blue eyes are surprisingly attractive.

"En fait, je voulais dire des musées et autres... Un peu de culture ne ferait pas de mal," he explains, catching me out with an embarrassing misunderstanding. I blush and am glad that the palm tree is between us.

"Est-ce que Louis **t'embête**[22]?" Poppy asks and squeezes in next to me.

She laughs boisterously and has already had a few glasses. She and Louis have been good friends for ages.

---

[21] brune – brown-haired
[22] embêter quelqu'un – to annoy someone

"Poppy, tu **gâches**[23] notre moment," Louis says and grins.

I'm still embarrassed by my excuse. Is he flirting with me or not? I decided to leave them alone and go to the dance floor. Dancing is always good. At some point, Poppy joins me.

"Louis est **mignon**[24], non? Tu ne l'aimes pas?" she shouted to me through the music.

"Oui, il est beau... Mais je sors d'une longue relation. Et je ne peux pas m'engager dans quelque chose de nouveau maintenant, parce que..."

"Tu n'es pas obligée de l'**épouser**[25] tout de suite!" Poppy interrupts me, laughing and dances away from me. I remain a little frozen. She is right... So, when the whole group is

---

[23] gâcher – to spoil, to mess up
[24] mignon – cute
[25] épouser – to marry

standing in front of the bar after closing time, Louis comes to me again.

"Tu n'aimes donc pas les hommes bruns? Que penses-tu des cheveux blonds ou noirs? Penses-tu que les cheveux blonds m'iraient bien?" he asks with a sympathetic, deep voice and an expectant smile on his face. I can't help but laugh. This time, he's flirting, I'm sure of it. So, I listen to my heart and do something I have never done before:

"Viens avec moi! Je vais te montrer ce que j'aime," I whisper in his ear. He looks as if he hadn't expected this reaction. Now he comes closer to me, puts his hand on my neck, and gives my lips a tender kiss.

"Où allons-nous?" he asks.

"Allons chez moi?" I suggest confidently, even though inside, I'm still entirely beside myself. Was that really me, or am I acting like I am in a

26

film? No, it's real. Then I think of Andrew. It's funny. We're not together anymore, but I feel a little like I'm cheating on him. I'm almost angry that I feel like that. Andrew is in the past. So, I'm doing this. I'm free, and I can do what I want. With that in mind, I pull the first man I meet after Andrew. We drive to my flat; Poppy and Claire know about it, so they stay in the bar for a while out of consideration.

After the flat door is locked, our lips hang on each other, our clothes fall, and we rush into my room. As we stand naked in front of my bed, it occurs to me that I haven't done one bit of exercise in the last few months. I try to push the thought aside and consider myself beautiful.

"Tu es belle," Louis says as if he has read my thoughts and runs his big hands over my body. I kiss him and let my hands slide over his arms, chest, and face.

We have passionate sex. Afterward, we lie in bed for a while and we talk for hours on end. Slowly, we both get tired, so I ask Louis one more favour as it is something important to me when having a one-night stand:

"Demain matin, tu dois être parti avant que je ne **me réveille**[26]," I whisper before he laughs and gently strokes my hair behind my ear.

"Ok, si c'est ce que tu veux..."

We sleep together, and the next morning, he is gone.

A few days after the night with Louis, I take another man home with me. This time, it was a friend of Claire's, a Portuguese DJ, who kept giving me glances from the DJ booth while I was dancing. I hesitated a little but then boldly approached him.

---

[26] se réveiller – to wake up

My newfound love life is crazy and exciting. I have fun and am getting so used to having purely physical bedtime stories that I am almost embarrassed by my actions. My innocent naivety amuses Poppy and Claire.

"**Même**[27] ma tante en sait plus que toi sur la vie amoureuse moderne, **bien qu'elle fasse l'éloge de la virginité tous les dimanches à l'église**[28]." says Poppy as we cook together on the Sunday evening before my first day at work.

"Hé, laisse-la tranquille." Claire interjects.

"Avant ce **connard**[29] de Andrew, elle était dans une autre relation de longue durée, non? Lily n'a jamais eu l'occasion de **se défouler**[30]."

---

[27] même – even,the same

[28] bien qu'elle fasse l'éloge de la virginité tous les dimanches à l'église – even though she praises virginity every Sunday in church

[29] le connard – idiot, jerk

[30] se défouler – to let off steam

"Exactement... Et ce n'est pas comme si je ne connaissais pas les **coups d'un soir**[31]. C'est juste que je ne l'ai jamais **envisagé**[32] pour moi," I say to defend myself.

The night with the DJ was also very nice. Everything seemed simple, uncomplicated, hot, and exciting simultaneously. I enjoy my freedom.

"Demain matin, tu dois être parti avant que je ne me réveille," I said.

"Si c'est ce que tu veux..." And the DJ was also gone in the morning, even though he left me a sweet message with his number.

---

[31] coups d'un soir – one-night stand
[32] envisager – to consider

# Chapter 3

Then comes the first day at the new company. I'm so nervous that I wake up at five in the morning and can't get back to sleep. Outside, the birds are chirping as if they are having a singing contest. I press my pillow on my head and close my eyes, but my thoughts go crazy.

I was in my old company for years. I knew my field exceptionally well. However, the biggest clients were a dental association, a commercial company, and a hairdresser with a penchant for creative hairstyle names. So, I know how to design teeth and make people want a Hairy Potter haircut. But at Celuxe, the clients are much more modern: from hip bars to big, world-changing NGOs. I don't know if I'm up to it. I have respect for the new job. And the many new people. After all, good relationships with relevant colleagues are worth their weight in gold. I have high expectations of myself and want to shine in my new role without being labelled 'the girlfriend' again.

But lying in bed and thinking about it forever doesn't help either. So, I get up and do a little morning yoga. I turn on a video of my old yoga teacher from my backpacking trip through Southeast Asia. Hearing her voice immediately calms me.

"**Inspire**[33] profondément et expire. **Détends**[34]-toi. Tu n'as rien d'autre à faire maintenant."

Before I met Andrew, I did yoga every day. I loved stretching and being so flexible! Why did I stop doing that? Why do some women disappear in their relationships? From a distance, it feels like I've been fused with Andrew for the last few

---

[33] inspirer – to breathe in
[34] détendre – to relax, to loosen

years and that I can only now breathe on my own again. Feel myself again. Me. Lily. Alone.

"Pénétrez à l'intérieur de vous-même. Laissez les pensées aller et venir."

Andrew was a somewhat jealous, controlling man (how ironic that he ended up cheating on *me*), but it was still my responsibility to shape my life. I had handed it over to him. It won't happen to me again. I come first now. I am me. And I want to be seen for that.

"Et maintenant, accueille ce jour. Aujourd'hui. Pas demain, ni hier. Maintenant. Chaque jour est une nouvelle chance."

I grimly do a sun salutation and decide that this will never happen to me again. I will never restrict myself like this again. I am me, no one's other half!

"Bienvenue, bienvenue. Nous sommes heureux de vous **accueillir**[35] chez Celuxe. Ici, nous sommes une famille, une famille qui ne **cesse**[36] de s'**agrandir**[37]. Et vous êtes nos bébés, tout juste **nés**[38]. Des bébés **de tous horizons**[39]. Cette semaine, le **sein maternel**[40] d'Celuxe vous **nourrira**[41]...."

I look around cautiously and try to find out if anyone else finds this welcome speech strange. A young woman with dark skin and flashing eyes catches my gaze, and we both look away quickly to avoid laughing out loud. The so-called 'newbies' sit on far too tiny, hip stools in the office lounge while Thibault, a platinum blonde man

---

[35] accueillir – to welcome
[36] cesser – to stop, to cease
[37] agrandir – to enlarge, to expand
[38] être né(e) – to be born
[39] de tous horizons – from all directions, from all over the world
[40] le sein maternel – the maternal breast
[41] nourrir – to feed, to nourish

with countless piercings on his face, looks theatrically into the distance. A presentation of photos from company events is running behind him, but I am far too fascinated by Thibault's sparkling outfit to pay much attention to it. The morning passes quite quickly. We play ice breaker games (I haven't done that in ages), are given a tour of the company (which has state-of-the-art facilities), and get to know the department heads from the different areas, although, of course, we are constantly told that there are no hierarchies.

"Vous devez moins les considérer comme vos **patrons**[42]... mais **davantage**[43] comme vos grands frères et sœurs..." Thibault explains.

"Qu'en est-il du **PDG**[44]?" asks the woman with flashing eyes. "C'est comme notre père?"

---

[42] patron – boss, employer
[43] davantage – much more
[44] PDG – CEO, managing director

Thibault, who has just shown us the games room where we can play table tennis, among other things, between our meetings, is a little upset.

"Le PDG... Monsieur Dupont... ne doit jamais - au grand jamais! - être appelé ainsi!" he says angrily.

He looks around anxiously as if this Monsieur Dupont could come around the corner at any moment. We look at each other in amazement, and Thibault forces himself to smile again.

"Mais vous ne le voyez probablement pas **souvent**[45] non plus. Monsieur Dupont est un homme très **occupé**[46]. Je suis l'un des **rares**[47] à travailler aussi **étroitement**[48] avec lui. Je suis quasiment sa seconde **main**[49]."

---

[45] souvent – often
[46] être occupé – to be busy
[47] rare – rare, occasional
[48] étroitement – closely
[49] main – hand

The tour continues in the afternoon. My head is already buzzing from so many names and new information. At Celuxe, almost all 100 employees seem to be happy. There is talk about healthy communication and being part of 'Pizza Friday'.

"Tous les vendredis, nous nous réunissons pour manger une pizza. C'est même recommandé dans notre **code de conduite**[50] comme événement pour notre culture d'entreprise."

"Code de conduite? Que devons-nous savoir **à ce sujet**[51]?" a man with a long beard asks and grins.

"Nous apprécions beaucoup que les employés soient plus que de simples collègues. Notre directrice des ressources humaines dit que l'on

---

[50] code de conduite – code of conduct
[51] à ce sujet – regarding this

est plus **performant**[52] quand on **se sent bien**[53] dans son environnement social. C'est pourquoi nous **essayons**[54] de **traiter**[55] chaque collègue avec **amitié**[56]. Nous ne sommes stricts que dans les relations amoureuses dans le travail. C'est trop **distrayant**[57]."

I like the attitude of - 'Never fuck the company'. It is what I have decided to use for my new beginning. We are making name tags for our places in the office (yes, really, making!) when there is a brief interruption to Thibault's welcome day, which is obviously planned down to the last detail. An attractive man, maybe around 30, but

---

[52] performant – efficient, high-performing
[53] sentir bien – to feel good
[54] essayer – to try
[55] traiter – to treat
[56] amitié – friendship
[57] distrayant – distracting

with the calmness of an old Zen master, suddenly approaches him from behind.

"Salut, comment ça va?" he says simply.

Thibault, who has just coloured in a flower on his name tag, jumps up, startled, and turns around.

"Tu dois être Jacques, non?" he asks after he has regained his composure.

The newcomer named Jacques nods and looks around, amused. I want to brush my hair behind my ear, but my hands are full of glue because I put glitter on my name tag.

"Apparemment, je n'ai pas encore manqué grand-chose." Jacques says and grins.

"Tu es **en retard**[58]," Thibault says, unable to avoid an indignant undertone.

---

[58] en retard – late

"Mon vol a été retardé. Et je croyais qu'il n'y avait pas de 09h00 à 17h00 chez vous?" says Jacques grinning. Even though I find him rather cheeky, I can't help but admire his composure. Our eyes meet for a brief moment, and my stomach warms. Jacques is strikingly tall, with a dark complexion and black hair. His eyes are a beautiful shade of blue and seem friendlier than his tone.

"Il n'y en a pas non plus," growls Thibault.

"**Sauf**[59] la première semaine. Là, nous **attendons**[60] de la ponctualité!"

"**Désolé**[61], je ne le savais pas réalisé," Jacques says kindly.

"Tu es Thibaut, n'est-ce pas? **Superbe tenue**[62]!"

---

[59] sauf – except, apart from
[60] attendre – to wait, to expect
[61] désolé – sorry
[62] superbe tenue – stylish outfit

Thibault cannot hide that he is flattered by this compliment. Jacques sits down with the rest of the group. Against all expectations, he joins in, and his name tag becomes such a beautiful work of art that even Thibault is speechless. Nevertheless, I am thrilled when it is the evening, and we have finished for the day.

"Quelqu'un d'autre **a envie de**[63] prendre **l'apéro**[64] après le **boulot**[65]?" I ask my new colleagues.

"Bonne idée... au fait, je m'appelle Alika," says the woman with flashing eyes. She smiles at me.

"**Enchanté**[66], je m'appelle Lily. Je suis d'Angleterre. C'est maintenant ma troisième semaine en France. Et toi?"

---

[63] avoir envie de – to feel like, to want
[64] l'apéro – a pre-meal drink with friends (typically french)
[65] boulot – work, job (informal)
[66] enchanté(e) (… de faire votre connaissance) – Pleased (… to meet you)!

"Je suis arrivée **hier**[67]! Je viens de Dodoma. C'est la capitale de la Tanzanie. Y es-tu déjà allée?"

"Non, **malheureusement**[68] pas," I reply.

"Je ne suis **jamais**[69] allé en Afrique. Mais j'aimerais bien visiter tous les pays du monde... ou du moins tous les continents!"

As I say this, I am surprised by myself. But it's true: I loved travelling as a child. But since my journey through South-East Asia, I have only ever taken holidays in England. Always to the same lake.

We leave work and stand in the street. It is a balmy spring evening. A few other colleagues join us. Not a single one of us is from France. Celuxe's concept is to bring in a wide variety of

---

[67] hier – yesterday

[68] malheureusement – unfortunately

[69] jamais – never

people from all over the world to meet their standards of unconventionality and creativity. The company uses French as its language. We stand in a small circle, and everyone introduces themselves:

"Je m'appelle Mailin. Je viens de Shanghai. Je suis engagée comme rédactrice chez Celuxe. Avant cela, j'ai travaillé dans une entreprise à Montreal. Mais Montreal est une ville trop américaine et trop froide pour moi. Je préfèrerais découvrir Europe."

Another one speaks up; it's the one with the long beard:

"Je m'appelle Vincent. Je suis originaire de l'île de la Réunion. Mais j'ai grandi en Hollande. Au cours des dix dernières années, j'ai **travaillé à mon compte**[70] et voyagé dans toutes sortes de

---

[70] travailler à mon compte – to be self employed

pays **en tant que nomade numérique**[71]. Depuis quelque temps, j'ai envie d'avoir à nouveau un **lieu**[72] de travail fixe. Et Paris **me plaît**[73], c'est pourquoi j'ai **postulé**[74] chez Celuxe."

I listen attentively. It is exciting to hear about the different life models of my colleagues. They have all done and experienced so much. I'm almost embarrassed that I've only lived in England so far, and I don't say that much at first.

"Je m'appelle Sarah. Originaire des États-Unis. Plus précisément: de Californie. Mais j'ai toujours eu trop chaud là-bas. Je n'aime pas trop transpirer, c'est pourquoi je suis ici maintenant."

The blonde, pretty woman from California laughs and the others join in her laughter. They are a

---

[71] en tant que nomade numérique – as a digital nomad
[72] lieu – place
[73] plaire à qn – to appeal to someone
[74] postuler – to apply for

likeable group. We decided to go to a small nearby bar where you can sit outside and order an aperitif and olives.

"Qu'est-ce qui arrive à Thibault? Il **perd la tête**[75]!" Vincent asks and laughs.

"Demain, il va faire danser nos noms ou quelque chose comme ça. Il croit qu'on vient de sortir de la **maternelle**[76] ou quoi?"

"Honnêtement, je pense que ça va être vraiment **dur**[77] après la première semaine," Alika says, looking serious.

"J'ai entendu dire que Celuxe voulait être assez performante, même si cela ne semble pas être le cas lors de l'onboarding."

---

[75] perdre la tête – to lose one's mind
[76] maternelle – nursery
[77] dur – hard

"Oui... Vous avez vu comment Thibaut a réagi quand Alika a demandé à voir le PDG? Ce Monsieur Dupont doit vraiment être un **sale type**[78]..." says Mailin. She has a cool accent and a beautiful, broad smile.

"Je ne sais pas" I say. "Jacques est arrivé en retard comme ça. Le premier jour! Et il ne lui est rien arrivé non plus... ils ne peuvent pas être aussi stricts."

Just at that moment, Jacques comes by and spots us. He has a supple, elastic gait, as if he didn't have a single problem in the world. He casually winks at us and continues walking. That suits me fine because, somehow, I find him arrogant. (But maybe I'm also jealous because his name tag has become much nicer than mine. Thibault did well to treat us like kindergarten children). But then Alika calls him:

---

[78] sale type – nasty guy

"Salut Jacques. Nous sommes en train de parler de notre premier jour ici. Viens nous **rejoindre**[79]."

He pauses, turns around, and comes closer with a broad smile. He pulls up a chair from the next table, orders a beer, and squeezes between Alika and me, of all people.

"Alors je suis **reconnaissante**[80] de pouvoir commencer chez Celuxe," I say, and I mean it. It is, after all, one of the best advertising companies in Europe. And if Celuxe hadn't taken me, I'd probably still be sitting with my parents in the backwater that is home instead of drinking cocktails with people from all over the world.

"Attends de **rencontrer**[81] le vieux Monsieur Dupont..." Jacques says and slaps me on the shoulders. A little too hard. Ouch.

---

[79] rejoindre – to meet
[80] reconnaissante – grateful
[81] rencontrer – to encounter

"Pourquoi? Est-ce que tu l'as déjà rencontré?" I ask curiously while rubbing my shoulder. In the meantime, the others start a conversation about the French club scene.

"Rencontré? Je suis quasiment son nouvel assistant personnel."

"Son assistant? J'aurais plutôt pensé que tu faisais... quelque chose de créatif."

"Je l'ai fait aussi... mais chez moi, en Provence, j'y avais un atelier. Mais j'ai dû le fermer. On ne vit pas que de l'art," Jacques tells us.

He sounds slightly bitter but more authentic than his post-pubescent appearance at Celuxe. And I am impressed. I enjoy my graphic designer job, but I also used to want to be an artist, and I know how difficult that is.

"Je suis désolé," I say. "Alors comment es-tu arrivé ici?"

"Le job m'est ...comment dire... **tombé dessus**[82]. Et **j'avais besoin de changer d'air**[83]. **Séparation**[84] difficile."

"Moi aussi!" I shout excitedly, only to bite my tongue. A break-up is not exactly the coolest thing in the world to have in common right now. Jacques laughs. He raises his glass.

"À la liberté," he says, and we toast.

"Et maintenant, que fais-tu de ta liberté nouvellement acquise?" I ask him after we have both sipped our drinks.

"**Baiser**[85] et peindre," he says.

"Je n'espère pas en même temps," I reply, and we both laugh.

---

[82] tombé dessus – stumble upon
[83] j'avais besoin de changer d'air – I needed a change of scenery
[84] séparation – separation
[85] baiser – to shag (informal)

"Et toi...? Qu'est-ce que tu fais en tant que **célibataire**[86]?" he asks.

"Je ne sais pas encore... j'ai fait du yoga aujourd'hui pour la première fois depuis des années."

"Oh vraiment? Ma mère est professeure de yoga. J'ai dû pratiquer des asanas dès mon **enfance**[87]. Celuxe est originaire **d'Inde**[88]."

"C'est beau! J'adore l'Inde!"

"Moi aussi... Le chaos, la **foule**[89], **la bonne bouffe**[90]... Je veux refaire un voyage en Asie du Sud-Est bientôt."

"Je veux faire ça aussi," I say dreamily. "Se promener à nouveau. Rencontrer de nouvelles personnes. Faire *vraiment* connaissance avec

---

[86] célibataire – single
[87] enfance – childhood
[88] Inde – India
[89] foule – crowd
[90] bonne bouffe – good food (informal)

quelqu'un. Au lieu de parler tout le temps du temps qu'il fait."

"C'est juste une façon poétique de dire que tu veux aussi baiser."

I snort, laughing into my glass. In a way, he's right. I enjoy my freedom and my affairs at the moment. I find Jacques attractive, but I won't do anything with him. All for my new rule, 'Never fuck the company'.

# Chapter 4

The evening passes as quickly as the day, and after a few drinks, the mood among my new colleagues is quite boisterous. Alika and I meet by chance in the ladies' room at a late hour, where she winks at me:

"Jacques te plaît, non?" she asks.

"Hmm... peut-être," I say and hiccup. Oh, oh. That was the last cocktail for today. I don't want to turn up on the second day of work with a hangover, even though we'll probably just have to play Mario Kart.

"Et tu lui plais aussi... ça se voit tout de suite." I look at her in the mirror. She blurs a little before my eyes. I shrug my shoulders.

'Never fuck the company', I'm sure I'll have to explain. If only I had stuck to this principle when

I met Andrew at the old company...I would have been spared a lot.

"Ah, tu sais... j'ai une théorie à ce sujet... Si c'est vraiment juste du sexe, alors c'est bon. C'est même excitant, parce qu'on peut se voir **en cachette**[91] entre deux réunions pour **se bécoter**[92]. C'est juste que ça devient difficile quand les **sentiments**[93] entrent en jeu."

She's right. Relationships at work only get complicated when feelings come into play, especially when they are unbalanced, like with Andrew and me. It gets weird when one has more or different interests in a relationship than the other. As colleagues, you can't avoid each other. You see each other every day, and break-ups can also have a direct impact on your work situation. The best example was how my boss

---

[91] en cachette – in secret
[92] se bécoter – to snog
[93] sentiments – feelings

treated me. Not objectively, but I'll never repeat that again. So, I answer confidently:

"C'est bon, Alika. J'ai déjà deux beaux hommes avec qui ce n'est pas compliqué. Je n'ai pas besoin d'un troisième."

In fact, I texted Louis an hour ago to come and pick me up, and he should be there any minute. We go back to the terrace, where Jacques is flirting with Sarah. But when I come closer, he immediately interrupts the conversation and looks at me.

"Je dois y aller," I say and give a friendly wave. At the same time, out of the corner of my eye, I see Louis drive up in his car.

**"Reste**[94] encore un peu," Jacques says, and I notice that Sarah is not at all pleased that she suddenly doesn't get all his attention anymore.

---

[94] rester – to stay, to remain

"Non, je veux bien dormir cette nuit pour bien commencer la nouvelle journée de demain. Comme ça, je pourrai mieux admirer la tenue **scintillante**[95] de Thibaut!"

With these words, I turn around, give Alika a peck on the cheek and get into the car. I am aware that Jacques can see me doing this. But the days of slut-shaming are over, and honestly, the freedom to do what I want is worth any bruised male ego.

Fortunately, Louis had disappeared when I woke up the next morning. I do a few yoga sun salutations despite a slight hangover. Then I hurry to get ready for work. I drink a large coffee and eat a piece of toast. But even then, the bathroom is still occupied. That must be Claire - Poppy is not usually awake this early. And she

---

[95] scintillante – sparkling

doesn't take such excessively long showers either. I knock impatiently on the door.

"Est-ce que je peux aussi aller dans la salle de bain maintenant? Prendre une douche ou au moins **me brosser les dents**[96]?" I call impatiently. My need may be small, but still, it makes me grumpy.

"J'ai encore besoin d'un peu de temps, **ma chérie**[97]. Va donc te brosser les dents dans la cuisine," Claire calls cheerfully from the shower. Of course, I need my toothbrush first, which is in the locked bathroom, but I don't want to wait any longer. I wash in the kitchen, but I can't get the smell of smoke from the bar out of my hair. Without further ado, I buy a toothbrush and toothpaste on my way to work and brush my teeth in the ladies' room. This early in the morning, there's no one at Celuxe yet - except

---

[96] se brosser les dents – to brush one's teeth
[97] ma chérie – my darling

maybe the newbies, and I suspect some of them are struggling with their hangovers and won't exactly be over-punctual. So, when I come out - still five minutes before Thibault's appointed time - I'm pretty relaxed and all the more surprised when I unexpectedly bump into someone and drop my little toothbrush bag.

"Pardon," I mumble and pick up my toothbrush and toothpaste.

"**Dehors!**[98]" says a barking voice. I look up, startled, and stare into the ice-blue eyes of a huge, older man. He stares at me so angrily that I get goosebumps. Usually, I'm not one to keep quiet. But suddenly, I can't get a single word out.

"Dehors ou j'appelle la police!"
"Mais... je…"
"Tu n'entends pas! Sors de là!" he suddenly shouts.

---

[98] dehors! – Out!

"Nous ne sommes pas une **association de sans-abri**[99]!"

I hastily collect my toothbrush and leave the company with shaky knees. Outside, I lean against the wall, my heart pounding. What was *that about*? I haven't felt like this since I was caught stealing raspberries as a child by our bad tempered neighbour. Luckily, Alika is just arriving. She looks as beat up as I feel, and I assume she partied late last night. But she smiles when she sees me.

"**Tu as une mine affreuse**[100]!" she shouts.

Then she looks at me worriedly.

"Ça va?"

---

[99] association de sans-abri – homeless association
[100] tu as une mine affreuse – you look terrible

I'm just about to tell the story when suddenly Jacques comes in. Suddenly, I'm embarrassed about how I'm behaving.

"Oui, tout va bien. C'est juste que quelqu'un vient de me **crier**[101] dessus. J'ai juste eu **peur**[102], c'est tout."

"On t'a crié dessus?" Jacques asks, having overheard my words.

"Cela doit signifier que le vieux Monsieur Dupont est ici aujourd'hui."

Monsieur Dupont? Our CEO? My heart is in my mouth. If this was the first meeting with my new boss...

---

[101] crier – to scream, to shout
[102] peur – fear

"Des yeux **bleus glacés**[103]? Près de deux mètres de **haut**[104]? A l'air d'un chef de la mafia Française?" Jacques asks.

I nod.

"Oui. C'est Monsieur Dupont."

Alika grabs me and wants to pull me along with her.

"Allez... il est presque neuf heures," she says.

I'm reluctant.

"**Il m'a mise à la porte**[105]," I say hesitantly.

"Pourquoi?"
"Parce que je me suis brossée les dents dans les toilettes."

---

[103] bleu glacé – ice blue
[104] haut – tall, high
[105] il m'a mis à la porte – he kicked me out

I am grateful to Jacques and Alika for not laughing or asking why.

"Thibaut m'a dit hier que pendant un certain temps, des sans-abri dormaient la nuit dans l'entreprise. Ils ont en quelque sorte '**craqué**[106]' le **code d'accès**[107]," Alika explains.

"Quand il a vu ta brosse à dents, il a dû penser que tu avais fait de l'entreprise ton **domicile nocturne**[108]," Jacques adds.

"Oh," I say. The fact that the boss mistook me for a homeless person when we first met doesn't exactly reassure me now.

"Ne t'inquiètes pas," Jacques says and looks at me with a calm gaze.

"Je vais lui parler."

---

[106] craquer quelque chose – to crack something

[107] code d'accès – access code

[108] domicile nocture – night shelter

Alika pulls me in, and a new day begins.

Welcome Week continues over the next four days. Even though I keep looking around for Monsieur Dupont, fortunately, he doesn't show his face again. I also hardly see Jacques anymore. He nods at me when we run into each other in the corridor, but he is rather cold when we talk. I don't know why. Thibault is also a lot more restless than yesterday and seems to be under tension. I suspect he is like this because the CEO is now in the house. So much for the corporate culture. Everyone I have met so far has lived by the friendly interaction. The boss is the only one I haven't had this impression of so far. But, apparently, the others feel the same way, and there is a different atmosphere when Monsieur Dupont is in the office. Accordingly, we don't play or do handicrafts like on the first day, and there are no more theatrical speeches from Thibault. Slowly, we are separated as a newbie group and introduced to our respective areas.

There is a lot to learn. On Friday, I got my first assignment - to design a poster for Celuxe because a rebranding is coming up.

I'm looking forward to the task but also feel incredibly pressured. After all, all my new colleagues will see the result of this assignment.

# Chapter 5

I am glad the week went by so quickly and that it is finally the weekend. It was a lot to take in, and I needed time to process it.

"Tu veux venir danser avec nous ce soir?" Poppy asks.

"Il y a une nouvelle **boîte**[109] qui a ouvert."
I shake my head.
"Non, je ne suis pas un fan des boîtes de nuit."

In fact, what I'd really like to do is rest. Maybe call my best friend, Kate, or my parents.

"Depuis quand ça?" grins Poppy.

"Oh, allez.." Claire says and winks at me.

"Le DJ portugais va mixer..."

---

[109] la boîte – club, box (informal)

I shrug my shoulders. Somehow, I don't feel like going out today.

When they are gone, I open my laptop, read a few emails, and scroll through my social media feeds with a cup of café au lait in my hands to keep up to date with the lives of my friends in England. Suddenly, I spill half my drink over the bed in shock. Andrew is engaged. My ex. *Engaged*?! I didn't even know he had a new girlfriend! It's not like I have any interest in that cheating ass anymore. But seeing it so black and white that he's getting married is more intense than I would have thought. After all, we were a couple for years. Unwillingly, tears spring to my eyes. I want to stop them, but I have no chance. And then I really start to cry. Since the breakup, I've been nothing but angry. Now I'm... finally sad. I don't just think of all the bad things Andrew has done. But also all the good things. I mourn his humour, his down-to-earthiness, and even his cooking skills. I tear open the window and listen to the mild spring rain drumming on the roofs of the surrounding houses. It smells good, familiar, and new at the same time. My old life with Andrew, which was so good for so long, plays out in my mind's eye. At the same time, I see the rooftops of Paris in front of me, with all the wonders and secrets that still await me. I suddenly feel my legs and how they are firmly planted on the ground. I am here in Paris. This is what I have decided. This is my life. And then... the sadness stops. Curiosity about the future has taken over. I dry my last tear, and suddenly, my heart feels so light. Sometimes, it has to hurt again so that you can really let go. I put on my favourite music and started dancing around the room. It doesn't bother me in the least that I'm alone. I'm still dancing when I hear the girls coming home. They are giggling and have a few friends with them.

"Tu **es encore éveillé**[110], ma chérie!" Claire says and grins as I hop towards her dancing.

"Dormir, je pourrai le faire quand je serai **morte**[111]!" I shout and pull her into me. One by one, the other people enter the room and are infected by Claire's and my dancing mania.

"Nous t'avons **amené**[112] quelqu'un," Poppy shouts and pulls the Portuguese DJ behind her, who smiles at me a little shyly. The fact that he regularly gets the crowds dancing is surprising, as he's pretty stiff in the hips.

"Cette soirée est bien meilleure que celle de la boîte," exclaims a girl with red cheeks.

"D'où vient ta **bonne humeur**[113]?" Poppy asks curiously.

---

[110] être encore éveillé – to still be awake
[111] morte – dead
[112] amener – to bring
[113] bonne humeur – good mood

"Je suis juste tellement reconnaissante que ma vie m'ait amenée à Paris!" I call out and enjoy the moment.

We dance until it gets light, and when all the party guests have left, Poppy, Claire, and I lie down in my bed and sleep until late afternoon.

Accordingly, I go back to work on Monday feeling refreshed.

**"Qu'est-ce qui ne va pas chez toi**[114]**?"** Alika asks curiously.

"Je me sens juste bien... Libre!" I reply and sit down at my desk. I have a thousand ideas about the poster and the rebranding for Celuxe and even work into my lunch break to be ready for the pitch in the afternoon. Usually, I would be very nervous, but today, I feel like nothing can

---

[114] Qu'est-ce qui ne va pas chez toi? – What's wrong with you? What is the matter with you? What is going on with you?

rattle me. As I entered the meeting room, I smiled at those present: Alika, Jacques, Thibault, a colleague I haven't met yet, and my team leader. Jacques doesn't look up; he is doodling on his drawing pad.

"Et Lily, qu'as-tu **prévu**[115] pour Celuxe?"

I plug in my laptop and show a presentation of my designs to those present.

"J'ai pensé qu'il serait bon d'utiliser un design **sobre**[116]. Pour contraster avec **l'arrière-plan**[117] abstrait."

I show my three drafts and receive appreciative murmurs. Even Jacques has stopped doodling.

"C'est celui que je préfère," says my team leader.

---

[115] prévoir – to plan
[116] sobre – modest, sober, simple
[117] à l'arrière plan – in the background

"Pourrais-tu le **rédiger**[118] et me l'envoyer?"

"Oui, bien sûr!" I say and am pleased that she likes my design.

"Tu as vraiment du talent," Alika says and nods at me appreciatively.

Bang. Suddenly, the door slammed open so violently that we all flinch. Monsieur Dupont enters the room. Silence. The tension of my colleagues is physically palpable to me. In contrast to his loud appearance just now, Monsieur Dupont now moves slowly and deliberately. He prowls around like a big cat in the jungle and finally focuses on my presentation.

"Qu'est-ce que c'est?" he asks in his critical voice, looking at one of my drafts. So far, he hasn't looked at me, and I wonder if he will

---

[118] rédiger – to write

70

recognise me from the toothpaste incident and kick me out again right away.

When no one says anything, I clear my throat.

"Mes **dessins**[119] pour **l'affiche**[120]. Pour Celuxe," I explain. My voice is unusually low. When he answers nothing, I add:

"Pour le rebranding qui doit **avoir lieu** [121]dans un mois."

"Et avez-vous pensé à demander à L'aubere?" he finally says.

Who the hell is L'aubere?!

"Hum."

---

[119] dessin – drawing
[120] l'affiche – poster
[121] avoir lieu – to take plce, to occur

My heart is beating like crazy. There is something about this man that absolutely terrifies me.

"Bien sûr que non. Les jeunes d'aujourd'hui ne s'intéressent plus au véritable art français."

Monsieur Dupont sits down, crosses his arms in front of his chest, and stares at me with his ice-blue eyes. I am speechless. What is this all about? I look around helplessly. Everyone looks away or down at the ground except Jacques. Our eyes meet. He gives me a gentle nod - it's hard to see. That gives me courage.

"Je viens d'Angleterre et je suis chez Celuxe que depuis deux semaines environ. Je ne sais pas qui est L'aubere," I say in my defence.

Monsieur Dupont and I look at each other. I still feel like I've done something wrong, but I stand as tall as I can at that moment.

"L'aubere est l'artiste française dont tu as utilisé l'image," Jacques explains gently.

"Tu dois lui demander les **droits**[122]. Bien sûr, ce n'est pas encore important pour un premier **jet**[123]. Seulement si on **imprime**[124]."

I nod shakily. That makes sense. I hadn't thought of that. I just used the footage I found on the cloud.

"Demandez à L'aubere," Monsieur Dupont repeats in his menacing voice.

"Mais à part ça, le projet est tout à fait utilisable."

*Quite useable?* I am so relieved that Monsieur Dupont is about to leave the meeting room that I can't get angry at his choice of words. Just

---

[122] droit – rights (here: image rights)
[123] jet – draft
[124] imprimer – to print

before he reaches the door, he pauses once more.

"Bonne journée!" he says goodbye in a still serious tone.

When he is outside, the mood changes instantly. Alika smiles at me sheepishly. My team leader exhales deeply.

Thibault jumps up:

"Tu as entendu? Ma chère, demande à L'aubere aussi vite que tu peux. Le patron se met **en colère**[125] s'il n'**obtient**[126] pas ce qu'il veut."

He *gets* angry? And what was he just now? A purring kitten?

With that, the meeting is over, and everyone hurries to their workplaces.

---

[125] en colère – angry, furious
[126] obtenir – to obtain, to receive

At the end of the day, I feel like having a drink. Bullshit, I need a drink! I have no idea how to get those rights. And if I don't get them, what happens then? Does Monsieur Dupont himself dismiss me because he doesn't get what he wants?

"Tu as envie d'un café? Peut-être même un avec un peu d'alcool?" I ask Alika.

"Hmm... oui. J'aimerais bien prendre un verre avec toi, mais..." she says and looks past me.

"Alika, si tu n'as pas le temps, ce n'est pas **grave**[127]."
"Tu es sûre? Parce qu'en fait, j'ai un rendez-vous ce soir..."
"Bien sûr! Vas à ton rendez-vous. Je comprends!"

Alika smiles at me sheepishly and then adds:

---

[127] grave - serious

"Mais demain, nous ferons quelque chose ensemble. J'ai appris quelques gros mots français, spécialement pour Monsieur Dupont!"

Jandirk and Mailin have already left, and Sarah and I never really warmed to each other. I have a feeling she can't stand me. So, all that's left for me to do is ask Jacques. I would also like to thank him.

I find him at his workstation with a furrowed brow over a large spreadsheet filled with numbers.

"Je crois que c'est l'heure d'apéro ..." I say lovingly as I lean against the door frame.

"Viens, je t'invite!" I give him my best smile - which is not easy because inside, I am still angry with Monsieur Dupont.

"Pas aujourd'hui, je dois finir ça.." Jacques replies.

"Allez, une bière dans notre bar préféré."

"J'ai dit non!" He briefly looks up at me and underlines his answer with a definite look.

"D'accord, d'accord. C'était juste une question."

I stand still for a moment but say goodbye when nothing more is said. I am a little disappointed. I thought his support in the meeting room had made us something like accomplices. Maybe I was wrong, and it was nothing more than a nice gesture between colleagues.

"Alors, bonne soirée..." I say goodbye more formally and leave the room. But my thoughts are still on our short conversation. It annoys me that he treated me so coldly.

# Chapter 6

Instead of sitting in the bar, I go to the small coffee shop opposite. I'd rather just order a tea because I've spontaneously decided to visit the nearby yoga studio later. Staying sober is perhaps the wiser choice. It's cosy here but not kitschy. Quiet, but with pleasant background noise. You can certainly work well here, I think to myself.

After a while, the door opens, and Jacques, of all people, walks into the café. The shop area is so tiny that we can't pretend we haven't seen each other, but we try anyway.

Jacques unpacks a pad and scribbles on it. Since my mobile phone has run out of battery, I sip my tea and content myself by looking out the window. Stubbornly in the other direction. As if he still has to work...

"Ici."

Jacques suddenly puts a piece of paper on the table and snaps me out of my thoughts. I look suspiciously first at him, then at the sheet. It is a pencil drawing.

"C'est moi..." I am surprised to see.

"Tu regardes avec colère par la fenêtre," Jacques says.

"C'est beau..."
"*Tu* es belle."

"Hum... merci," I reply, slightly embarrassed.

"Tu es... vraiment talentueux!"

"Désolé pour tout à l'heure au bureau," Jacques says after a short pause.

"Être ici me stresse. Je ne voulais pas **me défouler sur toi**[128]."

He sits down next to me.

"Être chez Celuxe te stresse?"

"Oui... et ici à Paris. J'ai de mauvais souvenirs de cette ville."

"Tu es déjà venu ici?"

"Oui... plusieurs fois quand j'étais enfant. Mais c'était il y a longtemps. Parlons **plutôt**[129] de toi," he says just when things are getting exciting.

"Il n'y a rien de passionnant à dire sur moi. Je suis encore en train de découvrir ce que je veux vraiment faire dans ma vie et ce que je ne veux pas faire..."

"C'est **pourtant**[130] la chose la plus excitante qui soit. Imagine que certaines personnes vivent toute leur vie sans jamais le savoir."

---

[128] se défouler sur qn. – to take it out on someone
[129] plutôt – rather, instead
[130] pourtant – however, yet

"Peut-être que c'est même parfois plus confortable," I say and look outside thoughtfully. The past few months' emotional ups and downs have been exciting but far from comfortable.

"Quand j'ai eu 17 ans, j'ai quitté l'école," Jacques tells me.

"Mes parents **étaient horrifiés**[131]. Mon père en tout cas. J'ai cru à l'époque qu'il me **déshériterait**[132]. Ma mère s'est habituée... Je te l'ai dit, elle est professeur de yoga. Une femme **détendue**[133]. J'ai d'abord fait du cirque. C'était tout sauf agréable. Mais c'était la meilleure période de ma vie. Nulle part ailleurs je n'ai autant appris sur les gens."
"Tu as fait du cirque?!"

---

[131] être horrifié(e) – to be horrified
[132] déshériter – to disinherit
[133] détendre – to relax, to loosen

I would have expected a lot. But not this. Jacques starts laughing at my look.

"Pendant un an seulement. J'étais quasiment l'homme à tout faire avant de **me lancer**[134] dans l'art. Si tu veux, je t'invite au cirque un jour. Il y en a un en ville en ce moment."

He looks at me in a friendly way. Is this an offer between work colleagues or an invitation to a date? I can't tell at the moment. At the same time, I hear a reasonable voice in my head commanding emphatically: Never fuck the company, Lily. Jacques and I will not do acrobatics in the circus or in bed! But how do I tell him that? Do I even have to?

Before I can even react, fate takes over: Louis enters the café, and our eyes meet.

---

[134] se lancer – to throw oneself into something

"Hé Lily! Salut! Qu'est-ce que tu fais là?" he interrupts the conversation with Jacques. He sits with us without being asked, and I take the chance not to have to answer Jacques. I hug him in greeting, and he kisses me on the forehead. After that, the moment is comical. I introduce them to each other and try to build up a conversation until Jacques puts on his jacket, looks at Louis and me, and declares that he has to go.

"Jaques, ton **tableau**[135]!" I call out when he is already halfway to the door outside.

"C'est un **cadeau**[136] pour toi," he says, leaving the café without turning around again.

I remain seated with Louis and have a strange feeling in my stomach.

---

[135] tableau – painting
[136] cadeau – gift

"Je crois qu'il **est tombé amoureux**[137] de toi, Lily," says Poppy with her mouth full at dinner. I have just come in from yoga, and after such a long day, I am happy that Claire has cooked.

"De quoi tu parles?" I say, and I help myself to a portion of pasta.

"Louis! Je ne sais pas ce que tu as fait. Mais il n'arrête pas de parler de toi. **Franchement**[138], c'est assez **énervant**[139]."

"Je suis désolée... j'ai aussi **remarqué**[140] qu'il veut plus que moi. Je crois qu'il veut une relation."

"Alors, qu'est-ce qui t'en **empêche**[141]?" Claire now interferes.

---

[137] tomber amoureux – to fall in love
[138] franchement – frankly
[139] énervant(e) – annoying
[140] remarquer – to notice
[141] empêcher – to prevent

"Louis est gentil. Mais je n'ai tout simplement pas envie d'avoir une relation en ce moment."

"Donne-lui donc une chance. Tu ne peux pas rester célibataire pour toujours," Claire says.

"C'est à moi que tu dis ça?" I answered seriously, but amused at the same time.

"Les filles. Arrêtez de vous disputer. Tout le monde n'a pas la chance d'avoir trouvé la partenaire de sa vie dès la vingtaine," Poppy says and grins cheekily at us.

Poppy has been with her girlfriend for two years now, and it is the most loving, low-conflict relationship I have ever seen. At least, that's how it looks from the outside. But I just don't want a relationship right now, neither low- nor high-conflict.

"Je me concentre actuellement sur ma carrière. Je me **mets à mon compte**[142]. Je n'ai pas de temps pour les hommes," Claire says.

In fact, Claire has just started a delivery service pastry shop. The production facility is in our kitchen, which is why it smells like cake here all day. I have long since given up cooking. Claire now provides us with a delicious daily dinner out of gratitude—or guilt.

"Et j'ai trop de plaisir à être seule en ce moment. Je ne veux donc pas du tout avoir de temps pour les hommes." I justify myself and eat my pasta.

---

[142] mettre à son compte – to go freelance

# Chapter 7

The next day, the next problem is already waiting for me at Celuxe. The answer to my email from L'aubere has arrived.

"Veuillez ne pas utiliser ma photo pour l'affiche. **Veuillez agréer l'expression de mes salutations distinguées**[143]."

Bummer. I have already continued working with the firm conviction that I will get an acceptance.

"Je dois utiliser une autre image," I report meekly to my team leader.

"Mais Monsieur Dupont voulait celle-ci," she replies.

---

[143] veuillez agréer l'expression de mes salutations distinguées – Yours sincerely

"Eh bien, ça ne va pas vraiment lui **briser le cœur**[144]. S'il en a un. Il l'a juste trouvé 'tout à fait utilisable'."

My team leader looks at me with wide eyes. Then she starts to laugh bitterly.

"Ma chère, sais-tu combien de temps j'ai travaillé ici avant de recevoir un 'tout à fait utilisable' de Monsieur Dupont? Quand il dit ça, ça veut dire en fait qu'il trouve ça très bien."

"**Vraiment**[145]?" I ask doubtfully. Somehow, I can't imagine that.

"Oui. Alors obtiens ces **droits d'auteur**[146]! Tu dois utiliser *cette* image. Pas une autre."

---

[144] briser le cœur – to break the heart
[145] vraiment – really
[146] droits d'auteur – copyright

She sends me back to my desk, and I email L'aubere again - this time in a downright submissive tone. She writes back just as quickly:

"J'ai dit non! Je ne veux rien avoir à faire avec les sociétés de publicité. Pour **aucun argent**[147] au monde. Et maintenant, laissez-moi tranquille!"

Hm. That's a clear message. What am I supposed to do now? I quickly searched for 'L'aubere' on the internet and discovered that luckily for me, she's at an opening in town tonight. Asking her in person is my only chance.

I throw on my smartest dress, force Alika to come with me, and we are at the gallery on a small side street in Paris at eight o'clock on the dot. We are almost the first ones there, and after sneaking in through the back door, we now try to

---

[147] aucun argent – no money

look at the paintings by modern French artists as inconspicuously as possible.

"Au fait, tu as un plan?" Alika asks. She is still in a bad mood because her date yesterday didn't go well. And that's despite the fact that there's complimentary champagne here.

"Mon plan est d'engager une conversation charmante avec L'aubere. Puis de lui demander à nouveau ses droits, si elle m'aime bien."
"Et si elle ne t'aime pas?"
"Elle finira par m'aimer. **Il faut**[148] juste que tu restes loin d'elle."
"Ha-ha. Mais sais-tu au moins **à quoi elle ressemble**[149]?"
"Eh bien... non... mais je vais le **découvrir**[150]!"

---

[148] il faut – one must
[149] à quoi elle ressemble – what she looks like
[150] découvrir – to discover

"Comment vas-tu faire pour **passer inaperçue**[151]? Veux-tu parler à chaque personne individuellement? Tu veux crier leur nom? Veux-tu faire peindre des étiquettes avec le nom de chaque personne ici?"

I sigh. Alika is not helping me much right now.

We stop before a painting we both like, which briefly silences our conversation. It is a drawing of a woman in the circus, probably made with watercolours.

"Ça vous plaît?"

Alika and I turn around at the same time.

"Jacques! C'est de toi?"

He nods and points to the nameplate under the painting: Jacques Kumari.

---

[151] passer inaperçu(e) – to go unnoticed

"Dis-moi, tu me suis?" I ask and smile weakly. First, the coffee, then the vernissage. Paris may feel small, but it is not small at all.

"Je pourrais te poser la même question," Jacques says and grins.

"Que faites-vous ici?"

"Lily s'est mis en tête de parler à L'aubere," Alika replies.

"L'aubere? C'est une vieille amie à moi. Des jours d'été parisien."

"Vraiment?" I ask excitedly. He could help me. But I am too proud for that.

All of a sudden, Jacques grins.

"Tu veux que je t'aide? Je pourrais simplement lui parler."
"Non, merci. Je me débrouillerai."
"Oh, allez."

"Non. Tu as refusé mon invitation à boire une bière..."

"Eh bien..."

Alika looks from me to Jacques, amused, and suddenly interrupts us:

"Les gars, je crois que L'aubere vient d'entrer."

"Comment le sais-tu?" I ask, looking at the young woman with the extravagant hat who has just entered the gallery.

"Le photographe a crié son nom," Alika replies.

L'aubere has already discovered Jacques.

"Jacques, mon cher," she calls and gives him a peck on the cheek.

**"Ça fait une *éternité*[152]."**

---

[152] ça fait une éternié – what she looks like

"C'est vrai. Ça fait vraiment longtemps qu'on ne s'est pas vus, Linda. Je crois que la dernière fois, c'était à la pool party, où tu étais tellement ivre, non?" he says and grins.

"Ssch. Mais pas ici! Et 'Linda' est morte depuis longtemps," says L'aubere, looking around anxiously. Then she spots Alika and me and gives us each a kiss, too.

"Dommage. Linda était **chouette**[153]," Jacques says, and I hope he shuts up immediately so I can finally ask Linda - or L'aubere - to sell Celuxe the rights to her picture.

But she doesn't even think about talking to me any longer; instead, flitting from one semi-celebrity to another and basking in the intrusive attention of the press. I help myself to the complimentary champagne throughout the evening and watch L'aubere like a vigilant

---

[153] chouette – cool, great, a treasure (informal)

tigress while Alika is bored and answers Jacques' questions about his artworks. She has to be alone at some point. Finally, L'aubere excuses herself and disappears to the toilet. This is my chance! I down the fifth glass of champagne and follow her to the toilet. L'aubere puts on her eyelashes, and I open my mouth to speak to her...

Uh-oh.

The last sip of champagne was too much.

Instead of going towards L'aubere, I run into one of the cabins and slam the door behind me. All the champagne I consumed tonight comes out in a gush.

"Uah. Tout va bien **là-dedans**[154]?" L'aubere asks, and I can only imagine the disgusted look

---

[154] là-dedans – in there

on her face as I hang over the bowl like a heap of misery.

"J'ai déjà été mieux," I say quietly and wipe my mouth with toilet paper.

"Ces événements sont toujours très **fatigantes**[155]. Tu n'es pas la première à finir **au-dessus des toilettes**[156]," L'aubere says, suddenly sounding more like a Linda.

"Tu as l'air d'aimer l'événement."
"Moi? Ah, je ne fais que donner aux gens le spectacle qu'ils souhaitent. C'est bon pour les **affaires**[157]. Mais chaque artiste le fait comme il l'entend. Jacques, par exemple, n'est pas comme ça. Il est toujours resté lui-même."
"Depuis combien de temps vous connaissez-vous?"

---

[155] fatigant – tiring, exhausting
[156] au-dessus des toilettes – above the toilet
[157] affair – business

"Depuis que nous sommes enfants. On a vécu brièvement dans le même **quartier**[158] avant que ses parents se séparent. C'est un bon **gars**[159]."

I can't believe I'm having a conversation with L'aubere through a closed toilet door - about Jacques, of all people.

"Tu sais... en fait, je suis là pour toi," I say carefully. It's now or never.

"Ils le sont tous, ma chère," she says, now sounding more like L'aubere again.

"Je travaille chez Celuxe. Nous nous sommes déjà entretenues par mail il y a quelques jours. Mon patron adore ton art et c'est pourquoi j'aimerais te demander personnellement quelles sont les possibilités pour que nous puissions utiliser ton image..."

---

[158] quartier – neighbourhood
[159] gars – guy (informal)

I press the flush and come out. I wash my face while L'aubere is still silent. I wait anxiously for her answer. She adjusts her hairstyle and gives me a look.

"Désolé, mais je ne peux pas faire ça, ma chère. Mes **valeurs**[160] sont plus importantes que ta carrière."

With these words, she leaves me alone. The mirror reveals my dishevelled reflection. My mascara is blurred, and my hairstyle is destroyed. I walk out dejectedly and look for Alika, who is talking to Jacques. This evening has been a disaster, and all I want to do is go home.

"Allons-y!" I suggest.

---

[160] valeur – value

"Qu'est-ce qui t'est arrivé?" Jacques asks amusedly and lets his gaze glide over my wild hair.

"**Ça ne te regarde pas**[161]," I hiss.

"Ça n'a pas marché?" Alika asks with compassion. At least her bad mood is gone.

I shake my head. What if they dismiss me now? Will I have to go back to England? Will I live with my parents again? Will I run into Andrew and his fiancé? Suddenly, I felt like the biggest failure in the world. Can't it just be easy for once?

I feel tears welling up in my eyes. I definitely don't want to be seen like this— I might even be crying in one of the press photos . I quickly leave the gallery with Alika by my side. I can feel Jacques' eyes on my back for a long time.

---

[161] ça ne te regarde pas – it's none of your business

"Je n'ai malheureusement pas **réussi**[162]," I confess dejectedly.

It's ten o'clock in the morning, and I'm facing my team leader. It's best to get it over with straight away. She shakes her head in disappointment.

"Qu'est-ce qu'on fait maintenant?" I ask her expectantly.

"Ce n'est pas à moi de décider. C'était le **souhait**[163] de Monsieur Dupont," she replies, looking thoughtfully through the window.

"Le mieux est d'aller le voir tout de suite et de lui dire."

---

[162] réussi(e) – successful
[163] souhaiter – to wish

# Chapter 8

The walk to Monsieur Dupont's office feels like walking into death row. My legs are heavy, and I don't really want to move forward. Before I knock, I take a deep breath. Then, once more. And again. I repeat this a hundred more times. Until I can't avoid it anymore because my colleagues are already looking at me strangely. Finally, I knock.

"**Entrez**[164]!" his barking voice commands.

I enter and am surprised to find not only Monsieur Dupont but also Jacques. Obviously, the two had just been in a heated debate because they both have red faces and look past each other.

"Que voulez-vous?" Monsieur Dupont asks.

---

[164] entrer quelque part – to go in somewhere

"Je viens pour l'image de L'aubere. Malheureusement, je n'ai pas pu en obtenir les droits," I say as quickly as I can. It's like taking off a plaster: It must be done promptly. If you do it too slowly, it's just excruciatingly painful. I expect screams, bursting veins, spraying spit. But Monsieur Dupont just looks at me with a furrowed brow.

"De quoi parlez-vous? L'aubere m'a écrit ce matin pour me dire que Celuxe pouvait l'utiliser." "Celuxe a...? Quoi?"

I am confused. Monsieur Dupont's eyebrows draw together angrily. I glance at Jacques, who makes a twitching head movement towards the door.

"Oh. Oui. C'est vrai. Alors je vais **me remettre au travail**[165]," I say and turn around carefully.

---

[165] se remettre au travail – to get back to work

"Le premier mot **sensé**[166] qui sort de votre **bouche**[167]," Monsieur Dupont says, and I leave his office quickly before he says anything else mean.

I sit down at my desk and spend the next few hours concentrating on work, even though I still don't quite understand who saved my ass here.

"Jacques," I call out as we meet in the corridor just before closing time. I pull him into a small storage room, which smells of old detergent and dust.

"Euh," he says and looks around with amusement.

"Je dois te **remercier**[168]," I murmur.

---

[166] sensé – sensible
[167] bouche – mouth
[168] remercier – to thank someone

"Pour ton **aide**[169] avec L'aubere." I look into his confused face and quickly kiss him on the cheek. Even though it is only a moment that my lips touch his cheeks, it feels strangely familiar.

"Hum. Ne **te méprends**[170] pas, je n'ai rien contre le fait d'être embrassé par de belles femmes dans des chambres **obscures**[171]. Mais ce n'était pas du tout moi avec L'aubere," he says carefully.

"Mais alors, pourquoi a-t-elle changé d'avis?" I ask, confused.

He shrugs his shoulders.

"Peut-être qu'elle t'aimait bien."

Suddenly, I realised how cramped it was here. We have only a few centimetres of space

---

[169] aide – help
[170] se méprendre – to be mistaken
[1/1] obscures – dark

between us. Neither of us moves to leave the room again, but we look deeply into each other's eyes.

"Il fait **plutôt**[172] **chaud**[173] ici," I say, suddenly desperate to break the intense silence.

"Lily," he says softly and slowly reaches out to brush a strand of hair behind my ear. His touch triggers goosebumps all over my body. "**Tu m'as plu**[174] dès le **début**[175]." I back away but bump into a shelf. My heart starts beating like crazy. What is happening here?

"J'ai essayé de **t'éviter**[176], mais d'une certaine manière, tu me rends les choses assez difficiles," he says quietly. Well, that explains

---

[172] plutôt – rather
[173] chaud – hot
[174] plaire à quelqu'un – to please someone
[175] début – beginning, start
[176] éviter – to avoid

why he has sometimes been cold towards me. He actually tried to avoid me.

"Jacques," I say.

"Nous travaillons ensemble."

"Je sais..."
"Ils ne trouvent pas les relations de travail bonnes ici," I whisper.
"C'est ce que Thibaut a dit le premier jour."
"Je pense qu'un peu de risque ne fait que rendre la chose plus excitante," he says.

He takes a step closer. I can feel the heat radiating from him. I greatly desire to snuggle up to him, let my body melt into his, and think of nothing more. But a little voice in my head warns me. And suddenly, it becomes too tight for me here. I have to get out! Breathe! I gently push him back and yank the door open. Bright sunlight streams towards me, and I stumble out of the chamber. Today, I've had enough of Celuxe.

And of men. I leave the company without turning around again. Behind me, Jacques gently closes the door.

# Chapter 9

The weeks pass, and spring turns into summer.

"Allons à la **plage**[177]!" Poppy shouts on the first really hot day of the year.

"Oh oui, je nous prépare vite fait quelques snacks!" says Claire, and I know I have no other choice. But a trip to the beach doesn't sound so bad. Mainly because I've been working very hard for the last few weeks. After the project with L'aubere - which was supposed to be my exam - one project after the other followed. I rarely saw Monsieur Dupont after that. Fortunately.

My life was also very eventful in other ways. After the fiasco at the gallery that night, I stopped drinking. Instead, I now do yoga almost every day and have even started jogging again. I don't

---

[177] plage – beach

think I've ever been this fit in my entire life. The kilos I put on after my break-up with Andrew are falling off all by themselves, and I just feel good in my skin. I still go to parties and meet up with the Portuguese DJ occasionally. I ended the thing with Louis. It was heartbreaking.

"Louis, on ne devrait plus se voir," I said.

"Mais Lily..."
"J'ai simplement l'impression que nous voulons des choses différentes."
"Lily, s'il te plaît, donne-moi une autre chance. Je peux **m'améliorer**[178], je te le **promets**[179]."
"Il ne s'agit pas de **devenir meilleur**[180]. Tu es bien comme tu es. Je ne veux simplement pas de relation. Et je ne veux plus te faire de mal."

It went on like that for another hour. He didn't want to understand. It wasn't easy and

---

[178] s'améliorer – to improve
[179] promettre – to promise
[180] devenir meilleur – to get better

heartbreaking to get the words out. But I know (especially after the separation from Andrew) that it is better for both of us this way. I remain true to myself and choose the life I really want deep inside me. And it's only fair to him to meet someone he wants and who can give him what I can't or don't want.

Besides, I feel bad for Poppy. She can't meet up with the two of us now.

"Maintenant, il vient toujours **pleurer**[181] chez moi. Il ne peut tout simplement pas s'en sortir. Il a un **chagrin d'amour**[182]."

"Je suis désolé, Poppy. Je ne pensais pas non plus que ce serait si difficile pour lui."

"Maintenant que c'est fini avec Louis..." Claire interferes.

"Que penses-tu de Jacques?"

"Nous ne sommes que des collègues."

---

[181] pleurer – to cry
[182] chagrin d'amour – heartbreak

"Mais ne serait-ce pas bien si..."

"Non!"

Although Jacques is really attractive, I want to follow my newly discovered path. No more starting a relationship at work, not like with Andrew. After all, I've been doing so well since taking control of my life after my relationship with Andrew. I have learned a lot through this new chapter, and I want to use these insights to never bend again. I am pleased with the way I am—single.

Jacques and I don't have much to do with each other anymore. Only superficial, collegial contact at Celuxe. In a way, I'm glad because I don't want to risk something like the situation in the storeroom again. I just want to protect myself in case something happens again, as it did with Andrew. So, a few sunny hours on the beach will do me good.

Sometimes, Alika joins our housemate excursions, but she has just fallen in love and is often busy elsewhere.

My birthday is coming up at the end of August. My parents and my best friend would love for me to come home, but I'm not ready for that yet. I don't want to interrupt my Paris flow now.

On my birthday, I treat myself to a second-hand shopping spree. I buy myself a new dress and a pair of shoes that are far too high, and I stroll straight home in them. When I unlock the door, it smells deliciously of cake, as always, but it's quiet. Poppy and Claire may still be out. I go into the kitchen, hoping for a cupcake, and experience Déjà Vu:

"Surprise!!"
"Bon anniversaire, Lily!"
"Félicitations!"

## "À la tienne[183], Lily!"

The kitchen is bursting with people. Around ten happy faces grin at me: Poppy, Claire, and many of my work colleagues. Alika, Mailin, Vincent, Sarah and - Jacques.

I am taken aback when I discover him. He looks at me a little sheepishly. Then I see Sarah snuggled up close to him. They must be here together. I notice all this in a split second. I greet my guests and let a birthday song wash over me, then I grab Claire by the hand and pull her into my room.

"Pourquoi as-tu invité Jacques?" I ask without much ado.

"Qu'est-ce qui te fait penser que c'est *moi*?" she replies and crosses her arms in front of her chest in a huff.

---

[183] à la tienne – cheers (when toasting)

"Parce que Poppy a accepté que je ne veuille que m'amuser. Alors que toi, tu veux toujours me mettre dans une relation stable, comme une nonne catholique!"

"D'accord. Mais ce Jacques... il a quelque chose. Vous iriez tellement bien ensemble!"

"Claire!"

"Je dis juste... Et tu pourrais aussi ne faire que t'amuser avec Jacques, si c'est si important pour toi."

"C'est compliqué. Nous travaillons ensemble. En plus, il a dû avoir une histoire avec Sarah."

"Cette blonde? Sarah m'a tout de suite **paru**[184] **antipathique**[185]."

I start laughing, and we go back to the kitchen. For the rest of the evening, I managed to avoid

---

[184] paraitre – to seem
[185] antipathique – unlikeable

Jacques. Eventually, however, we meet over chips.

"Si ma présence te **met mal à l'aise**[186], je m'en vais," he says.

"Tout va bien."
"Ton amie Claire n'a pas accepté un 'non' comme réponse."
"**Je te crois sur parole**[187]."

We smile at each other momentarily, and then suddenly, Sarah comes dancing up. She snuggles up to Jacques, puts his hand on her hip, and looks at me with a broad smile and slightly narrowed eyes. She is about to open her mouth to say something when she is interrupted by Poppy's loud voice:

---

[186] mettre mal à l'aise – to make someone feel uncomfortable
[187] je te crois sur parole – I take you at your word

"C'est parti, les gars. La nuit ne fait que commencer et il y a un pub quiz chez, *Le patio*' ce soir," she calls and herds the pack together.

Arriving at the pub, the group is divided into two teams. I find myself in one group with Poppy, Alika, Jacques, and a few others. Meanwhile, I am pleased to see that Sarah is in the other group and can only admire Jacques from a distance.

"Bienvenue à tous! Etes-vous prêts!?"

A few people bawl drunkenly in response. I'm glad that I don't drink anymore and look around amused.

Then the moderator calls the first question into the microphone:

"Mesdames et Messieurs, je vous demande votre attention! Notre première question pour ce soir est: Quelle est la capitale de l'Inde?"

Jacques and I look at each other and say the answer at the same time:

"New Delhi!"

We deliver the answer and earn applause and appreciative looks from our group.

"Absolument juste! 10 points pour vous!"

"C'était facile," Jacques says.

"Comme un jeu d'enfants!!" I say and stick my nose up in a playfully arrogant manner.

"C'est bon, on a compris. Maintenant, concentrez-vous à nouveau, les génies," Poppy says and grins.

"La deuxième question de la soirée: Quel est le nom de l'artiste qui s'est **coupé** [188]une **oreille**[189]?"

It's been a while since my last art lesson, but I haven't forgotten. Again, Jacques and I shout the answer at exactly the same time, as if we had rehearsed it in chorus beforehand: "Van Gogh!"

"Encore juste! Félicitations!" the presenter shouts, and Jacques and I give each other a high five.

I can't help but notice Sarah's sour expression. I have all the more fun for it. Question after question is asked, and it quickly becomes apparent: We win!

---

[188] couper – to cut
[189] oreille – ear

"Au fait, avez-vous encore besoin de nous?" Poppy asks as Jacques and I both shout the correct answer at the same time again...

"Nous **avons** simplement **de la chance**[190] aujourd'hui!" I say with a laugh. Poppy smiles back and goes to get another beer.

We win, hands down.

"Et les heureux **gagnants**[191] de la soirée auront droit à **une tournée de boissons**[192] gratuites! Félicitations!" the moderator calls out. Poppy collects the orders and goes to the bar.

"J'ai besoin d'un peu d'air," Jacques says and stands up.

"Je viens avec toi," I say and only now notice how hot it is in the pub.

---

[190] avoir de la chance – to be lucky

[191] gagnant(e) – winner

[192] une tournée de boissons – a round of drinks

We go together to the small backyard, where it is not much cooler, but at least we are spared the smell of beer and sweat.

"Tu n'étais pas mal," Jacques says and winks.

"Eh bien, toi non plus," I say amicably.

"Mais les questions étaient faites pour nous..."
"C'est vrai. Nous avons aussi beaucoup de choses en commun."

I then remain silent. Suddenly I realised that I was with Jacques. That tall, handsome man with warm eyes. We haven't been alone together for a very long time.

"Ce n'est pas sensé **être de la drague**[193]," he says apologetically.

"Tout va bien," I say quickly and somewhat embarrassed.

---

[193] être de la drague – to be a pickup line

"C'est vrai. Nous avons vraiment beaucoup de choses en commun."

"Au fait, je suis désolé..." he says softly.

"De quoi parles-tu?"

"L'histoire de **débarras**[194]."

"Oh... c'est bon."

"Non, ça ne va pas. Tu m'as dit de manière catégorique que tu ne voulais rien. Et je t'ai **harcelé**[195]."

"Tu ne m'as pas pressé!"

"Si, j'ai simplement mal compris tes signes. J'ai beau avoir trente ans maintenant, j'ai encore parfois du mal à comprendre les femmes."

I look at him long and thoughtfully. Inside, the bar is filled with loud laughter and music.

---

[194] débarras – storage room
[195] harceler – to harass

I wonder what would happen if I did try it with Jacques? Maybe it's not like with Andrew. Maybe it could be different. Maybe I've been far too uptight about this thing with Jacques. I wonder if I have been unfair to him.

Maybe I'm getting the 'never fuck the company' wrong? I don't know. I am unsettled and look at his beautiful face. Strands of his hair fly in the wind. Then I feel my heart quiver and my pelvic floor tightening. I have a desire for him.

Then, I think briefly of a conversation I had with Alika. She said that it only gets complicated with feelings. Maybe that's the key. Without further ado, I decided to reformulate my self-imposed rule. Sex is okay, but I don't want a relationship.

"Tu n'as rien compris **de travers**[196]," I whisper.

He looks at me in surprise.

---

[196] de travers – wrong, askew

"Maintenant, je suis encore plus **confus**[197]," he says.

I take a step towards him, and now we are as close again as we were in the storeroom. Finally, he understands. He gently takes my head in his hands, and we look deep into each other's eyes. The air between us breaks, and he kisses me tenderly. I have to stand on my tiptoes, but it still feels like I'm melting. Neither the Portuguese DJ nor Louis nor Andrew have ever aroused such physical feelings in me. I feel hot, and suddenly, it can't go fast enough. I embrace him and push myself against him. He moans softly and pushes me a little away from him.

"Attends," he says softly.

"Quoi?"

"Sarah."

---

[197] confus – confused

"Pourquoi?"

We are still standing close to each other. I kiss him again; Jacques laughs softly and cannot defend himself against me. But then a voice interrupts us.

"Qu'est-ce que vous faites?"

Sarah suddenly stands behind us and stares at us. Jacques and I dive apart.

"Qu'est-ce que tu fais, Jacques?" she says shrilly.

"Tu es ici avec *moi*!"

I look around uneasily and try to decipher the French sign hanging above the bicycle racks. Sarah is breathing heavily, and suddenly, I feel sorry for her.

"Je suis désolé, Sarah. **C'est de ma faute**[198]," I apologise and feel caught. I don't want it to get around at work.

"**Ne t'en mêle pas**[199]!" she hisses. Then she turns and runs away.

"**Zut**[200]. Je vais lui parler," Jacques says, and I nod. He gives me an apologetic look and follows her. I text Poppy and go home without saying goodbye. I'm annoyed. It has to be a secret. After all, I want to be seen at work for what I do, not for who I snog.

On Monday at work there is a small letter on my desk:

"Lily, le problème avec Sarah est **réglé**[201]. Je suis maintenant en **voyage d'affaires**[202] pour

---

[198] C'est de ma faute. – It's my fault.
[199] ne t'en mêle pas! – Don't get involved!
[200] zut – damn (informal)
[201] régler – to sort out
[202] voyage d'affaires – business trip

une semaine. Mais à mon retour, j'aimerais **reprendre**[203] la conversation là où nous nous sommes arrêtés la dernière fois. Peut-être dans un **endroit**[204] plus agréable cette fois-ci? Jacques."

I can't help feeling instantly warm at the thought of him. Maybe Alika is right. Maybe this is something you can do with work colleagues when there are no romantic feelings. And there aren't. It's still the same! But physically, I have never experienced anything more intense.

Once again, I would like to apologise properly to Sarah. I find her in the office kitchen making coffee. I would have expected her not to be particularly well disposed towards me, but she smiles broadly at me.

"Hé Sarah, tu as une minute?"

---

[203] reprendre – to resume
[204] endroit – place

"Pour quoi faire?"

"Je voudrais m'excuser."

"Tu veux donc t'excuser?" she says sweetly, and I already suspect that it's about to get unpleasant for me.

"Pour vous avoir **attrapé**[205]?"

"Non... donc..."

"Pour **avoir dragué**[206] mon date?"

"Non, je veux dire..."

"Alors ne le fais pas, Lily!"

She exuberantly takes her cup of coffee and stalks off. I look after her with a guilty conscience. In a way, she's right. I knew she was there that night with Jacques, but I kissed him anyway. Why does it have to get complicated now, even though I wanted to keep all feelings

---

[205] attraper – to catch, trap, or hold back
[206] draguer – to flirt

out of it? I'll get Alika and ask her for an emergency meeting.

"**D'abord**[207] Louis et **ensuite**[208] Sarah. **D'une certaine manière**[209], je fais constamment du mal aux gens qui m'entourent depuis que je **profite de la vie**[210] comme ça."

"Ce doit être la **punition de Dieu**[211]," Alika says and grins.

"Je suis sérieuse! Je ne veux pas **faire de mal**[212] à personne!"

Alika stops grinning and takes me in her arms.

---

[207] d'abord – first
[208] ensuite – then, afterwards
[209] d'une certaine manière – in a way
[210] profiter de la vie – to enjoy life
[211] punition de Dieu – God's punishment
[212] faire de mal – to hurt someone

"Je sais, ma chérie. Mais si tu **culpabilises**[213] maintenant et que tu ne t'amuses plus jamais, personne n'y gagne non plus. Pas vrai?"

"Probablement pas."

"Eh bien, justement. Alors profite juste de ton temps avec Jacques quand il sera de retour."

"Qu'est-ce qui t'a rendu si **sage**[214]?" I ask and give her a playful nudge with my elbow.

"L'amour, Lily, l'amour..."

---

[213] culpabiliser – to make someone feel guilty, to feel guilty
[214] sage – wise

# Chapter 10

The rest of the week goes by pretty quickly. Not least because our beloved CEO is back in the house and orders me, of all people, into his office. Although I have been working here for a few months now and always get good feedback from my team leader, I still suffer in agony when I *hear* Monsieur Dupont's name. I knock carefully and enter.

"J'ai besoin de vous pour un nouveau projet," he says, without even greeting me.

"Moi... ?" I stammer to myself. As always, my confidence fluttered out the window as soon as I spoke to Monsieur Dupont.

"Vous m'avez été recommandée."
"Moi? Vraiment?"
"Mais maintenant que je vous vois comme ça, je doute que vous y arriviez..."

"Si... Si. Je pense que je peux le faire. Alors, peut-être. Ça dépend. De quoi il s'agit?"

I bite my tongue. I have just made all the communication mistakes in the world with my insecurity.

"Vous devez pour cela laisser de côté tout autre projet sur lequel vous travaillez actuellement. C'est un projet qui a besoin de tout votre concentration."

"Je comprends."

"Et vous devez me montrer tous les jours vos derniers résultats."

"C'est bon."

"Et vous ne devez en parler à personne - à personne - Compris?"

"Oui!"

I am slowly becoming curious. This project must be really important. But why is Monsieur Dupont making such a big secret of it? And why does he turn away from me while he talks to me?

"Ma femme m'a **quitté**[215]."

Monsieur Dupont is still looking out of the window. He seems to find it very difficult to say that. But I am just as confused. Why the hell is he telling me this?

"Oh. Je suis désolé," I say slowly.

"Oui. Elle a simplement fait ses **valises**[216] et est partie la semaine dernière. C'est la deuxième femme qui me quitte."

I'm starting to feel uncomfortable.

"Mes enfants sont maintenant tout ce qui me reste. Mais ils ne veulent rien savoir de moi."

"Oh." What can you say to that? I can understand his children very well...

---

[215] quitter – to leave
[216] valise – suitcase

"Votre mission est de **concevoir**[217] quelque chose qui **montre**[218] à ma femme à quel point je l'aime."

"Ne serait-il pas plus simple que vous lui disiez simplement?" I ask cautiously. I think his proposal is the stupidest proposal since romantic comedies have existed.

"Si votre avis m'intéressait, je vous paierais pour parler, pas pour concevoir. Vous êtes la meilleure designer de la maison."

Finally, he turns around and stares at me again with his ice-blue eyes, so evil that I unconsciously sink into myself. I felt sorry for him briefly, but now that's over.

"J'ai ici des photos de ma famille. Vous pouvez les utiliser. Trouvez une idée."

---

[217] concevoir – to design, conceive
[218] montre – to show, demonstrate

He slides something across the desk, and I see a younger Monsieur Dupont with a happy boy and a little girl in his lap. There is a magnificent Christmas tree in the background, and Monsieur Dupont has a smile on his face for once. In another photograph, Monsieur Dupont, aged by several years, is seen with a cool-looking blonde woman on a plain background. Here, his features already show the beginnings of the bitterness that is so prominent on his face today.

"Et maintenant, partez!" he says. I hurriedly leave his office and sit down thoughtfully at my desk. I look at the photos for a long time, especially the Christmas photo. I wonder what happened to Monsieur Dupont that made him the way he is today. Then I got to work and started drawing the photo with the woman so I could animate it later. Every morning, my first trip is to Monsieur Dupont's office. He is not easy to please, and his comments are often bordering on insulting:

"Un enfant de maternelle peut faire mieux!"

Or:

"Vous **perdez**[219] votre temps et me faites perdre le mien."

And, the classic:

"Faites-le encore une fois. Et **vite**[220]!"

I swallow his spiteful comments and usually don't say anything back. What should I say? He is still the boss. On Thursday evening, however, I came home with tears in my eyes because Monsieur Dupont was particularly unpleasant.

"J'en ai marre de travailler pour des cons," I say to Claire and Poppy, who are cleaning up the kitchen together.

---

[219] perdre – to lose, waste
[220] vite – quickly

"Fais comme moi!" Claire says and puts a vase that was used as a beer mug back in its proper place.

"Et comment, **je dois me mettre à mon compte**[221]?"

"Exactement! Tu as des horaires flexibles et tu peux travailler où tu veux. Et le meilleur: tu peux choisir tes clients! Tu n'auras plus jamais à travailler pour des **connards**[222]!"

"Je ne sais pas. Je n'y ai jamais pensé," I say slowly.

"Alors il est temps! **De toute façon**[223], je trouve que tu travailles beaucoup trop," says Poppy. She has just two evening performances a week and earns her money doing God knows what.

---

[221] se mettre à son compte – to start one's own business
[222] connards – bastards
[223] de toute façon – in any case

"Et si je n'ai pas de **clients**[224]?" I ask doubtfully.

"Je serais ta première cliente!" Claire exclaims.

"Maintenant que les choses vont si bien pour moi, il me faut absolument un **site internet**[225] et des **cartes de visite**[226]! Et je ne vais certainement pas te traiter comme ton **connard de patron**[227]."

It makes me laugh. The idea that Claire would be anything like Monsieur Dupont is absurd.

"Merci les filles. Mais je crois que pour l'instant, je préfère rester à la sécurité de l'**emploi**[228]."

And on Friday, the redeeming words finally came from my boss:

---

[224] client – customer, client
[225] site internet – website
[226] darte de visite – business card
[227] connard de patron – bastard boss
[228] emploi – employment, job

"Celui-ci est tout à fait utilisable. Allez-y," he says, making a wagging hand gesture as if I were an annoying chicken he has to shoo away. No 'thank you', no 'well done', nothing.

I am so angry that I forget that he is my boss for a moment. I open my mouth to give him a piece of my mind. At that moment, he looked up, and the corners of his mouth twisted into a mocking smile.

"Oui, s'il vous plaît?" I stand there frozen. But I can't get a word out, making me even angrier. He seems to suspect what's going on inside me because he's still staring at me with that smug smile.

"Avez-vous encore quelque chose à dire?" he asks.

"Non," I say after a while, my voice so low that it can hardly be heard.

"C'est ce que je pensais."

I turn around and leave his office.

The only thing keeping me going this week is that Jacques returns at the weekend. He didn't write to me until Friday evening—not that I was waiting for a message from him—and we arranged to meet in a park on Sunday afternoon. If it had been up to me, we could have met right there in my bedroom, but I play the game.

# Chapter 11

Summer is slowly passing, and even though it is still warm, the first leaves are changing colour. Autumn has always been my favourite season, so I arrive with a smile.

"Tu as l'air heureuse," Jacques shouts as I come towards him with big steps.

"Je le suis **effectivement**[229]!" I reply, pushing all my worries with Monsieur Dupont aside for the moment. We stand facing each other for a moment, a little uncomfortably. How do we greet each other? Should we hug? Exchange kisses? After all, what we have is not a date in the classical sense. We decide on a bumpy hug.

"On se promène un peu?" Jacques finally asks me, and I nod.

---

[229] effectivement – indeed, really

"Alors, où étais-tu passé?" I ask to get the conversation moving.

"Ah, là et là. J'ai dû faire des choses," Jacques replies.

"Cela **semble**[230] mystérieux."
"C'était plutôt **ennuyeux**[231]. Monsieur Dupont me met pas mal de pression. Il y a beaucoup à faire."

Now, the conversation has landed back on our CEO. A wave of anger flows through my body whenever I hear his name.

"Je le **déteste**[232]," I say softly.

"Il est tellement **insolent**[233]."

"Hum... oui... peut-être," Jacques says.

---

[230] sembler – to seem, look
[231] ennuyeux – boring
[232] détester – to hate
[233] insolent – cheeky

"Tu ne trouves pas? Je ne comprends pas comment on peut être comme ça. Si méchant et pas un « s'il te plaît ». Pas étonnant que sa femme l'ait quitté. Je m'étonne même qu'il ait été marié! Deux fois même."

"Sa femme l'a quitté?" Jacques asks, surprised.

"**Bon sang**[234] - oui, mais ne le dis à personne. Il me l'a dit en secret. En fait, je ne dois le dire à personne."

"Alors pourquoi tu le fais?" asks Jacques.

"Quoi?"
"Pourquoi me le dire alors qu'il t'a demandé de ne le dire à personne?"

We stop. Jacques looks at me as if I have done something terrible.

---

[234] bon sang – oh dear (expression)

"Ecoute, Monsieur Dupont ne m'a pas vraiment bien traitée. Pourquoi devrais-je **garder**[235] ses secrets? Ce n'est pas comme si c'était ma meilleure amie ou quelqu'un d'important à mes yeux."

"Comme tu veux."

"Ecoute…" I say, and slowly, I get angry too.

"Parlons d'autre chose."

I want to go on, but Jacques holds me back by the sleeve.

"Attends.." he says.

"J'ai encore quelque chose à te dire."

"Quoi donc?"

**"Asseyons-nous**[236]**."**

He pulls me to a park bench. I feel quite uncomfortable. What's next? Jacques picks up a stick from the ground and plays with it.

---

[235] garder – to keep, store
[236] s'assoir – to sit down

"Il y a quelque chose que tu dois savoir sur moi avant que nous fassions... plus ample connaissance."

"C'est grave?"

"Hum... comme on veut."

I breathe in and out deeply. But I made a decision when I set off for France: Adventure: yes. But no complicated stories!

"Jacques," I say before he can start talking.

"Allons chez moi."

"Tu ne veux pas savoir ce que j'ai à te dire?"

"Je ne veux pas **rendre** les choses **plus compliquées**[237] qu'elles ne le sont."

He laughs softly and throws the stick away.

---

[237] rendre plus compliqué – to make things more complicated

"Regarde. Tu aimes la **liberté**[238], j'aime la liberté," I declare.

"Et nous venons tous deux de relations compliquées et ne voulons plus de cela," he says slowly.

"Et nous sommes attirés l'un par l'autre," I add.

"Les sentiments ne feraient pas que compliquer les choses."

"Alors on les laisse partir!" I shout and grin.

He looks at me seriously and then holds out his hand.

"Pas de sentiments," he says.

I lash out and shake his hand vigorously.

"Pas de sentiments," I repeat.

---

[238] liberté – freedom

That's exactly how I imagined it. I want my private life to be separate from my professional life. Then everything is easier, and I have what I want: objectivity at work. And a great time in bed with a hot guy who imagines the affair exactly as I imagine it. That way, it's perfect.

By the time we get to my house, it's already dark outside. Poppy and Claire are at the cinema, so we have the place to ourselves. We go into my bedroom, and Jacques looks around, amused.

"Je ne savais pas que tu aimais les boy bands Français."

"Ils étaient déjà là avant que j'**emménage**[239]!" I reply. For some reason, I didn't want to take the posters down.

"Oui, c'est ce que je me disais maintenant..."

---

[239] emménager – to move in

I throw a pillow at him, and Jacques deftly dodges it. He now comes at me, grabs me, and throws me onto my bed. I try to fight back, but he is clearly stronger. It's just a game, but that's what I like about us. It's fun to spend time with him...

"D'accord! On fait la **paix**[240]!" I call out, laughing, and he lets go of me. As tousled as we are, we look into each other's eyes.

"Tu as vraiment de beaux yeux," Jacques says softly.

"Hé! C'est trop **gentil**[241]. Beaucoup trop romantique!" I complain.

"Oui, mais c'est vrai. Tu veux que je t'insulte?"
"Oui! **Au moins**[242] un peu!"

---

[240] paix – peace
[241] gentil – nice, kind
[242] au moins – at least

"Eh bien, si ça t'**excite**[243]..."

I laugh again and watch Jacques looking at me intently.

"Bon, alors... tes **sourcils** [244]ne sont pas tout à fait symétriques!"
"C'est beaucoup mieux!"

He answers with nothing, and we finally kiss.

Later that night, we lie naked and exhausted next to each other. My flatmates have long since come home, and when I look at the clock, I am surprised to see that it is already three in the morning.

"Tu veux vraiment retourner en Angleterre?" Jacques asks after a while of comfortable silence, during which I almost fell asleep.

---

[243] exciter – to turn on, excite
[244] sourcil – eyebrow

"Je ne sais pas encore... Un jour sûrement," I say, yawning.

"Et toi? Tu veux retourner en Provence?"

"Pour l'instant, je préfère être ici... même si je ne peux pas faire **éternellement**[245] un travail où je ne peux pas être créatif. Mais voyons ce que l'**avenir**[246] nous **réserve**[247]."

"Avant, je voulais toujours savoir exactement à quoi ressemblerait mon année," I say.

"J'avais même une sorte de **plan quinquennal**[248]."

"Et aujourd'hui?" Jacques asks.

---

[245] éternellement – eternally

[246] avenir – future

[247] réserver – to set aside, reserve

[248] plan quinquenal – five-year plan

"Un plan de cinq minutes me **suffirait**[249]-il?" I reply and giggle.

"Comment ça t'est arrivé?"
"Les derniers mois ont fait **bouger**[250] les choses..."

I yawn again and notice how my eyes slowly fall shut.

"Avant de m'**endormir**[251], je dois t'expliquer ma règle la plus importante," I say wearily.

"On dirait qu'il y a un plan..." Jacques says with amusement.

"Le chaos de ma vie doit être bien structuré," I justify myself.

"Très bien. Quelle est la règle?"

---

[249] suffire – to be enough
[250] bouger – to movc
[251] endormir – to fall asleep

"Tu dois être parti avant que je ne sois réveillé le matin," I say.

Jacques straightens up with a jerk.

"Non," he says.

"Que veux-tu dire par 'non'?" I ask, confused, and sit up too.

"Je ne fais pas ça," Jacques says. He gathers his clothes and starts to get dressed.

"Qu'est-ce que tu fais?"

"Je rentre chez moi," he answers calmly.

I am confused. Until now, all the men have always agreed with the rule. It makes things so wonderfully uncomplicated.

"Regarde! Quand on se réveille ensemble, c'est trop intime."

"Ce que nous venons de faire était si peu intime."

"Tu sais ce que je veux dire. Il faut alors prendre le **petit déjeuner**[252] ensemble..."

"**Dégoûtant**[253]!"

"Et se brosser les dents..."

"Dégoûtant!"

"Et...-"

"Ce n'est pas grave. Je te comprends."

"J'espère que cela te **convient**[254] aussi comme ça?" I ask and put on a T-shirt as well. The beautiful mood has now completely vanished.

"Non, Lily. Pas de sentiments, tu te **souviens**[255]? Ne t'en fais pas. Tout va bien."

Fully clothed, he stands over me and looks at me with a look that strangely intimidates me. He gives me a fleeting kiss on the cheek.

---

[252] petit déjeuner – breakfast
[253] dégoûtant – disgusting
[254] convenir    to suit, agree with someone
[255] souvenir – to remember

152

"On se voit chez Celuxe," he says, quietly leaving my room. Totally confused, I am left alone and slowly sink back into my pillow. It smells like Jacques.

Evenings like these do not impact how we deal with each other at work. It's the same as always, collegial and friendly. Just as everyone expects at work. At the same time, it's exciting that no one knows about our shared private life. We often meet just as I want: it's uncomplicated, fun, and exciting. We get along, laugh, chat, and even become good friends. There's only one thing we never do: we never spend the night together. Before one of us falls asleep, the other one leaves. We don't talk about it; we just do it like that. A few weeks go by, and even though I have an insane amount of work to do, I'm doing really well.

"Qu'est-ce que tu fais ce soir?" Jacques asks me quietly one day, secretly stroking my bottom in our office kitchen. I smirk and look around, but we are alone.

"Je voulais essayer un nouveau studio de yoga aujourd'hui," I reply.

"**Dommage**[256]." Jacques says and puts on a small, mischievous smile.

"Maintenant, alors."
"Maintenant?"
"Lily, j'ai besoin de toi pour un projet important!"

He gently pushes me out of the kitchen.

"Ici? Tu es **fou**[257]?"
"Oui! Et oui!"

He pushes me into the storeroom we've been in before.

---

[256] dommage – pity
[257] fou – crazy

"On ne peut pas **fermer**[258] à **clé**[259] ici...," I say softly, but he has already started to kiss me.

"Je sais... c'est pour ça que c'est très **excitant**[260]," he whispers in my ear, and I need no further argument.

I had just pulled my T-shirt over my head when the storage room door was suddenly yanked open. It was Thibault in a particularly glittery outfit.

"Qu'est-ce qui se passe ici?!" he asks in his typically theatrical voice that can usually be heard throughout the office.

"Thibaut... s'il te plaît... **chut**[261]," we frantically try to appease him.

---

[258] fermer – to close
[259] clé – key
[260] excitant – exciting
[261] Chut – shush

"Pour une fois que je cherche l'**aspirateur**[262], je **tombe**[263] sur quelque chose de **tout à fait**[264].. *différent*!"

"S'il continue à crier comme ça, toute l'entreprise va l'entendre," I say to Jacques in a panic, already picturing in my mind how the whole staff sees me in my bra. Jacques grabs Thibault, pulls him into the chamber with us, and quickly closes the door. The three of us now stand huddled together in the dark, and it is even tighter than before.

"Qu'est-ce que c'est que ça? Qu'est-ce que vous voulez? Qu'est-ce que vous me faites?" Thibault exclaims anxiously.

"Thibaut," Jacques says in a surprisingly stern voice.

---

[262] aspirateur – vacuum cleaner
[263] tomber – to fall
[264] tout à fait – completely, totally

"Ferme-la une seconde, s'il te plaît."

Thibault gasps indignantly.

"Thibaut." I say urgently. "S'il te plaît, ne dis rien. Nous ne voulons pas que quelqu'un soit au courant de notre... euh... histoire."

"Mais l'amour au travail est **interdit**[265]!"

"Thibaut, s'il te plaît," Jacques repeats.

"Bien. Qu'est-ce que je reçois **en échange**[266]?"

"Qu'est-ce que tu veux?"

Thibault hesitates. When he starts to speak, his voice sounds strangely embarrassed.

"J'aimerais bien sortir avec vous..."

"Avec nous?" we ask in surprise.

---

[265] interdire – to forbid
[266] en échange – in return

"Oui, donc avec vous tous. Je ne veux pas de plan à trois, ne vous **inquiétez**[267] pas. Je veux sortir avec vous, les newbies," Thibault says.

"**Toute l'équipe**[268]. Jamais vous ne m'**emmenez**[269] avec vous quand vous allez boire un verre!"

Jacques and I exchange a brief, amused glance in the darkness. It's true Thibault is not exactly the most popular with his attention-seeking manner. But we also never thought he'd be up for a beer with his colleagues.

"Ok," Jacques says softly.

"C'est ce que nous allons faire. Pourquoi pas ce soir?"

---

[267] inquiéter – to worry someone
[268] toute l'équipe – the whole team
[269] emmener – to take along

158

Thibault nods enthusiastically in the darkness while I sigh. I can forget about my quiet yoga evening for the time being.

"Votre secret est en sécurité avec moi. Je suis une **tombe**[270]," he says conspiratorially.

Then he takes the hoover from the shelf, opens the door, and leaves us alone. We cling to each other and laugh for the first time for a few minutes.

The laughter fades when I am called to Monsieur Dupont's office in the afternoon. He's been abroad for a while now, so I've had an emotional break from his meanness. Now, however, my imaginative mind immediately kicks in: Did Thibault tell on us after all? Am I going to be fired and Jacques with me?

---

[270] tombe – grave

"Asseyez-vous," Monsieur Dupont says when I enter the office, I suspect something bad. So far, I have never been allowed to sit down. I've always just stood around a bit awkwardly.

"J'ai entendu quelque chose à votre propos," Monsieur Dupont begins.

My heart starts pounding. Oh no, oh no.

"Et c'est pourquoi j'ai décidé de vous **promouvoir**[271]."
"Je... quoi?"

I am completely baffled. Promoted?!

"Vous n'avez pas écrit dans votre CV que vous aviez un **poste de direction**[272] dans votre ancien travail."

---

[271] promouvoir – to promote
[272] poste de direction – managerial position

I don't know what to say. The management position in my old company was not worth mentioning. My only task was to explain our work processes to the new trainees. And how does he know that?

"Euh. D'accord. Merci," I stutter. The day I get a full sentence out to Monsieur Dupont will be a big day for me.

"Vous allez travailler très **étroitement** [273]avec moi."
"Oh. Euh. Super."

Nice, Lily? *Nice*? I'm really shining with my answers today...

"Le **service du personnel**[274] réglera le reste avec vous. Maintenant, partez."

---

[273] étroitement – closely
[274] service du personnel – human resources department

I get up, and even as I walk out, I realise that Monsieur Dupont didn't even ask me if I wanted to accept the promotion. It seems I have no choice. Should I be happy? More work and more Monsieur Dupont? But also new, exciting tasks - and more responsibility. Can I even do that?

# Chapter 12

In the evening, Jacques, me, and Thibault, who flutters between us like a little bird that can't hide his excitement, go for a drink in our bar with all our colleagues: the colleagues from the HR department and customer service, plus Mailin, Vincent, Sarah and Alika, who has brought her new boyfriend. It's a lovely evening, and I'm happy we're all spending time together again. Everyone has heard about my promotion by now.

"À la tienne, Lily!" my colleagues call and toast while I half-heartedly force myself to smile.

"Tu n'es pas contente?" asks Vincent, who always has a keen eye for the moods of others.

"Si... alors, eh bien..."

"Qu'est-ce qui se passe?" Vincent asks.

I look into his friendly eyes, and it bursts out of me:

"Je ne sais pas du tout si je peux le faire!" I burst.

Vincent laughs.

"Être promue par Monsieur Dupont signifie essentiellement que tu es une sorte de génie," he says calmly.

"Oh, **arrête**[275]!" I say, but I can't stop my cheeks from turning red with pride.

"Tu vas y arriver, Lily. Et si ce n'est pas le **cas**[276], il y aura un autre **moyen**[277]."

I nod. It sounds so simple. It was good to hear that.

---

[275] arrêter – to stop
[276] cas – case
[277] moyen – means, way, method

"Merci, Vincent. Tu es gentil," I say, already knowing I will miss him if I no longer work here one day.

Later, I go to the toilet with Alika and say "Ton **copain**[278] est **mignon**[279]!" I'm desperate to change the subject and stop talking about my promotion. Alika unwraps her lipstick and beams at me.

"Oui, je sais! J'ai encore du mal à croire que nous sommes ensemble..."

I wash my hands and try to straighten my hair. I want to tell her about the thing with Jacques. I like her. She's one of my closest friends here in Paris. And I know I can trust her. She would keep my secret to herself and not spread it around at work.

---

[278] copain – boyfriend
[279] mignon – cute, pretty, lovely

"Au fait, je dois **t'avouer**[280] quelque chose.." I say out of nowhere, and her eyes flash. We haven't seen each other for so long that I haven't had a chance to tell her the news with Jacques.

"Jacques et moi sortons ensemble..."

"Ha! Enfin! Je le savais!" Alika exclaims.

"Depuis peu... un **truc**[281] du genre 'Friends with Benefits'."

"Tout est simple, hein?" Alika says and winks at me.

"Oui, c'est vraiment bien comme ça!"
"Crois-moi, si c'est le bon, les sentiments ne changent rien au fait que c'est bien. **Au contraire**[282]. Et il y a aussi des relations amoureuses sans complications."

---

[280] avouer – to confess, admit
[281] truc – thing, stuff
[282] au contraire – on the contrary

"Oui... peut-être dans ton monde. Mais ne le dis à personne. Nous voulons le garder secret."

At that moment, the door of a toilet cubicle slams open behind us, and Sarah struts out. Of course. Only I can be that unlucky. Alika and I cast a quick glance at each other. I wonder how much she heard. She stands next to us and calmly washes her hands, dries them, and then heads for the door without saying anything. I'm already breathing a sigh of relief; then, she turns around again.

"Au fait, je me demande si ta relation avec Jacques a quelque chose **à voir avec le fait**[283] que tu aies été promu aujourd'hui," she says. "De quoi tu parles?" I ask.

"Ah, tu ne sais pas?" Sarah says and smiles at me smugly.

---

[283] à voir avec le fait – to have to do with the fact

"Je ne sais pas quoi?"

Sarah wraps one of her long blonde hair strands around her finger and is silent with pleasure.

"Écoute, Sarah, si tu as quelque chose à nous dire, dis-le. Sinon, laisse-nous tranquille," growls Alika, who, like me, has never been particularly fond of Sarah.

"Je pense qu'elle ferait mieux de demander à son 'friend with benefits'?" Sarah chirps and leaves us alone.

"Sarah est trop bizarre..." Alika says and frowns.

"Mais ne l'écoute pas..."

"Tu sais quoi? Je ne la crois **pas du tout**[284]. Je devrais peut-être vraiment parler à Jacques," I say thoughtfully. I remember our autumn walk.

---

[284] pas du tout – not at all

He wanted to tell me something. Maybe I should have just let him tell me.

We go outside, and I look for Jacques; he is chatting with Vincent. I point outside (ignoring Sarah, who is watching us gleefully), and he follows me out into the street. By now, it is winter, and France is anything but warm in winter. Freezing, we put on our jackets.

"Qu'est-ce qui se passe?" Jacques asks, looking at me questioningly.

"Si tu veux faire l'amour, trouvons un endroit chaud."

"Ce n'est pas la question," I say gruffly. Jacques' relaxed manner suddenly makes me angry.

"Mais?" he asks, casting a longing glance at the warm bar.

"Sarah a **découvert**[285] qu'il y avait quelque chose entre nous..."

"Oh. Et comment a-t-elle réagi?"

"**Toxique**[286]. Comme toujours."

"D'accord. C'est **stupide**[287]. Mais ce n'est pas la fin du monde. On va s'en sortir."

"Sarah a aussi dit que notre relation avait peut-être un **rapport**[288] avec le fait que j'ai été promue."

"Qu'est-ce qui lui fait dire ça?" Jacques says, but I know him well enough by now to see that he is nervous. Like a little schoolboy jumping from one foot to the other because he's been caught doing something.

---

[285] découvrir – to discover
[286] toxique – toxic
[287] stupide – stupid
[288] rapport – connection

"Je ne sais pas. J'espérais que tu pourrais me le dire?" I reply and cross my arms in front of my chest.

"Alors... j'ai une idée de ce qu'elle veut dire. Mais je ne pense pas que tu aies envie de l'entendre..."

"Dis-le-moi!" I say, a little annoyed.

"Ça va tout compliquer."

"C'est déjà fait!"

"Alors... ok... sûre?"

"Oui!"

"Ok... Monsieur Dupont est... C'est mon... père."

I stare at him. Is this a joke? It sounds like something out of a movie. *Lily, Monsieur Dupont is my father?*

"Lily, dis quelque chose."

"Si c'est vrai... pourquoi tu ne l'as jamais dit?"

"Parce que je ne voulais pas être connu comme le fils du connard. Parce que je ne voulais pas de traitement de faveur dans l'entreprise."

"Mais Sarah... C'est à Sarah que tu l'as dit?" I ask and have to laugh. The whole thing is absurd.

"Oui... à l'époque où j'étais en relation avec elle. J'ai trouvé ça juste."
"Et moi, alors?"
"Je voulais te le dire! Tu ne voulais pas l'écouter!"

We glare angrily at each other. Then I suddenly realised what Sarah meant. Does my promotion really have something to do with Jacques? Someone told Monsieur Dupont about my leadership position. And someone - I just remembered hot off the press - also recommended me to Monsieur Dupont at the time! Just like the thing with L'aubere, which he says he had nothing to do with. It must have all been Jacques.

"Tu te précipites chez ton papa pour parler de moi?"

"Non... je veux dire... oui... je lui ai peut-être dit quelque chose une fois..."

"Je le **HAIS**[289] et tu lui **racontes**[290] nos histoires de **lit**[291]?"

"N'importe quoi. Je lui ai simplement dit que tu avais du talent. L'histoire du leadership m'a échappée."

"Et L'aubere? Tu y as **mis ton grain de sel**[292] aussi?"

"Non... alors pas vraiment. Je lui ai juste montré des travaux de toi quand tu étais absente. Cela l'a **convaincue**[293]. Tu étais simplement **trop fière**[294] pour me demander..."

"Parce que j'aurais pu le faire toute seule!"

"Je voulais juste t'aider!"

---

[289] haïr – to hate
[290] racontre – to tell
[291] lit – bed
[292] mettre son grain de sel – to interfere, stick one's oar in
[293] convaincre – to convince
[294] trop fière – too proud

## "JE N'AI PAS BESOIN DE TON AIDE!"

I am so angry that I can't think straight. I feel like I've been thrown out of my own head. Like I need help. As if I couldn't do it alone. And then a man thinks he has to help *me*. Even though I'm so proud of what I've done on my own in my life. It's all an illusion. What is actually happening here? Why does it have to be so complicated?

Yet I like Jacques as a person, as a human being. He's a great lover and a funny friend, a perfect combination. But I don't like that he has his fingers in my career as my boss's son. I don't like that at all.

I storm off. As I run, I wrap my scarf around my neck. Now it's starting to rain. Everything is annoying me right now. The weather, the people, and this city bug me. A bus drives past me and splashes me with brown slush. I run after it, but the bus driver doesn't have the muse to wait for me and just drives away.

174

I stand at the bus station, shivering from the cold. Jacques joins me after a while and stands silently next to me. When he sees how cold I am, he wordlessly takes off his jacket and wants to put it on me.

"Je n'ai pas besoin de ta veste. Tu n'as pas besoin de m'aider," I say, still irritated.

"Tu n'as pas froid?" he asks.

Without an answer, he finally puts the jacket on my shoulders. I feel warm at the same time. It feels good. Reluctantly, I thank him:

"Hmm... merci."

We stand next to each other in silence for a while. I keep thinking about what he just told me, and it all makes sense. I could have guessed that Jacques was Monsieur Dupont's son: he told me he was often here as a child. His height and blue eyes also point to his relationship with

Monsieur Dupont, his surname, and dark hair from his mother's origins. The first woman to leave Monsieur Dupont. Not forgetting the photograph of Monsieur Dupont with his children: That must have been little Jacques and his sister. How had I been so blind?

"Lily, ça ne marche plus comme ça," Jacques says. I look out for the bus in panic, not wanting to hear what he has to say.

"C'est bon, je ne t'en veux plus," I say and play the cool one. I don't even know why I say that. Maybe because I like him, and I wish the thick air between us would disappear.

"Mais c'est exactement ce que je veux dire! C'est toi. Tu es en colère. Et tu as bien une raison de l'être!"
"Tu n'es pas très **doué**[295] pour te **défendre**[296]."

---

[295] doué – to be gifted
[296] défendre – to defend

"On ne peut pas faire comme s'il n'y avait pas de sentiments entre nous!"

**"La ferme**[297]!" I shout.

I don't want to hear it. It'll ruin everything. I wonder why I started this with Jacques. I thought I promised myself I wouldn't get involved with people at work. Now I have. Who knows what will happen now? Either I'll be the one among my colleagues who has a relationship with the boss's son and 'accidentally' gets promoted early or the one who turns Jacques down. I realise that I can't give up my pride. I want to be *me*. I want to be appreciated for who I am and what I can do. I don't want to be seen as 'the girlfriend of'. At the same time, I feel a painful stab in my chest when I think about having to give up what Jacques and I have together. It hurts.

---

[297] La ferme! – Shut up!

It doesn't help to hear what Jacques is going to say next.

"Nous passons presque tous les jours du temps ensemble. Nous **bavardons**[298], nous **rions**[299], nous faisons du yoga ensemble, nous cuisinons, nous **peignons**[300]... Je m'amuse avec toi comme je ne l'ai pas fait avec quelqu'un depuis longtemps."

"Nous sommes amis! Friends with Benefits," I declare in my distress.

"Je t'aime plus qu'un ami, Lily," he says softly.

"Et tu le sais aussi."

The bus! Thank God the bus is here.

---

[298] bavarder – to chat, gossip
[299] rire – to laugh
[300] peindre – to paint

**"Le marché entre nous**[301] était: pas de sentiments," I say sternly while the bus driver opens the doors and looks at me promptly. I turn to him again and give him back his jacket. It is still raining.

"Si tu ne peux pas de ça, alors notre relation est **terminée**[302] maintenant."

With these words, I get in. Jacques does not follow me. The bus drives off, and I slump down in my seat, tears streaming down my cheeks.

---

[301] le marché entre nous – the agreement between us
[302] terminer – to finish

# Chapter 13

The next morning, I am in bed with chills and a fever. It's the weekend, and even by Monday, I'm still not better and call in sick. Poppy and Claire lovingly provide me with soup and tea. Jacques calls a few times, but I don't pick up. Another conversation about feelings would be too much for me. Alika also calls me once or twice, but I am too weak to pick up. I don't feel like talking to anyone. For the first time since I've been here, I feel homesick. But is it homesickness? I don't exactly burst into joy at the thought of England. But right now, I don't want to stay here in Paris either. I want to sink into my bed.

"Ce n'est pas qu'une phase," Poppy explains to me after I've told the girls my woes...

"Oui, c'est tout à fait normal. Cela fait presque un an que tu es ici. Il est évident que ton pays **te manque**[303]," Claire adds.

"Je déteste la ville **tous les quatre matins**[304]," Poppy says and tries to make me smile.

"Et je veux **déménager**[305] au **Mexique**[306] au moins une fois par semaine," Claire also says.

I smile at that.

It's Sunday evening, and I feel physically well again for the first time in over a week. Tomorrow, I'll probably finally be able to go back to work, even though the thought of seeing Jacques and Monsieur Dupont makes me feel quite queasy. The ringing of the doorbell snaps me out of my thoughts.

---

[303] se manquer – to miss
[304] tous les quatre matins – all the time (expression)
[305] déménager – to move house
[306] Mexique – Mexico

"Qui **sonne**[307] à **minuit**[308] un dimanche?" Claire asks and frowns.

"Poppy, tu as encore commandé une pizza de minuit?" I ask with a grin.

Poppy shakes her head but happily runs out to open the door. We hear her talking to someone for a moment, and then she returns to the kitchen.

"Euh, Lily, Jacques est **dehors**[309] et veut te parler," she says.

"Ah bon? Mais je ne veux pas *lui* parler."
"Il dit que c'est très important."
"Ça m'est **égal**[310]."

---

[307] sonner – to ring
[308] minuit – midnight
[309] dehors – outside
[310] égal – equal, indifferent

"Chérie…" Claire says and gently puts her hand on my arm.

"Peut-être que tu devrais au moins écouter ce qu'il a à te dire."
"Non!"

Poppy stands unsteadily in the doorway, stepping from one leg to another.

"Qu'est-ce que **tu fuis**[311] **au juste**[312]?" Claire asks.

"Ne **recommence**[313] pas avec ça!" I shout angrily.

"Toutes les femmes qui ne croient plus au prince charmant romantique ne sont pas des personnages **tristes**[314]."

---

[311] s'enfuir – to escape
[312] au juste – actually
[313] recommencer – to start again
[314] triste – sad

"Romantisme ou pas, toi et Jacques, vous avez un **lien**[315]," Poppy says to my surprise. She usually always stays out of our conflicts.

"Et je pense qu'il **mérite**[316] d'être traité avec respect."
"Pourquoi êtes-vous de son **côté**[317]?"

"Nous ne sommes du côté de personne! Nous voulons juste que tu sois heureuse!" Claire exclaims.

I get up and leave the kitchen. To get to my room, I had to walk down the corridor. At the end of the hall, Jacques is standing in the doorway. It must be raining outside again because his cheeks are flushed, and his hair is wet. Although I'm angry, I can't help but notice how handsome he is. And how sad. And with a thud, it hits me: I've missed him. It even hurts my chest; that's

---

[315] lien – link, connection
[316] mériter – to deserve
[317] côté – side

how much I miss what's between us or what was. It's over; it's finished. I walk towards him with big steps.

"Lily, je suis content de te voir."

I slam the door in his face. Claire and Poppy stand behind me and look at me with open mouths. But neither of them dares to say anything. I go into my room and pull the covers over my head.

"Comment ça, Jacques est parti?" I ask. Alika and I have lunch together, and she brings me up to date.

"Je t'ai appelé plusieurs fois pour te le dire. Mais tu n'as pas répondu."
"Mais où est-il allé? Voyage d'affaires?"

"Non... Lily, il a démissionné. Il est retourné en Provence. Son vol est parti hier. La nouvelle s'est répandue dans l'entreprise qu'il était le fils du patron. Le savais-tu?"

I nod.

"Bien que je ne pense pas que ce soit la raison pour laquelle il est parti si vite," Alika says and looks at me thoughtfully.

I'm no longer hungry, so I left a large portion of lunch. I am ashamed of my childish behaviour over the last few days.

"Tout allait vraiment bien entre vous?" Alika asks, and I know she suspects something. But I can't talk about it right now and just make an ambiguous movement with my head.

The following two weeks are torture. Christmas comes and goes, but I don't get much out of it at all. Monsieur Dupont is as mean as ever. I work a lot and hard. In fact, I work all the time, even at weekends. I don't go out or party anymore. I'm not seeing any man. I don't recognise myself.

"Elle a un chagrin d'amour," I hear Claire say to Poppy in the kitchen one day.

"Je sais, mais c'est à elle de le découvrir..."
"Et elle travaille beaucoup trop."
"Probablement pour se **punir**[318]."
"Ou de **faire diversion**[319]."

I'm standing in the hallway waiting to pay the delivery guy and have to listen to my two flatmates' conversation. As I take out my wallet to pay the pizza delivery man, a crumpled business card flutters towards me. I pick it up in amazement. I vaguely remember my flight to Paris and my conversation with the old lady who kept talking about her granddaughter's problems. It seems as if it all happened in

---

[318] punir qqn./qqch. – to punish someone for something
[319] faire diversion – to divert attention

another life, yet it was less than a year ago. Without further ado, I dial the number.

"Bonjour, c'est Lily Kennett. Je connais votre grand-mère. Je suis graphiste," I say and ask myself at the same moment where I got my courage from.

"**C'est le ciel qui vous envoie**[320]! En ce moment même, je cherchais une graphiste."

We arrange to get to know each other. Afterward, I go to the kitchen and ask Claire straight out:

"As-tu toujours besoin d'un site web?"

"Euh. Oui, je dois..." she replies, puzzled.

"Alors j'aimerais le concevoir pour toi," I say.

"A prix d'ami, bien sûr."

---

[320] C'est le ciel qui vous envoie! – You're heven-sent! (expression)

"Je crois que maintenant elle a complètement **perdu la tête**[321]?!" I hear Poppy say as I leave the kitchen and sit down to work on my new projects. I grin.

Two customers quickly become three, and everything suddenly runs by itself. I set up my own business, and Claire helped me with all the bureaucracy. Currently, this means I work even more because I still have my job at Celuxe.

"Tu dois **démissionner**[322]!" she says one evening as we hang over the laptop in the kitchen late into the night.

"Je ne peux pas. Je viens d'être promue," I say and continue typing while she rests her head on her hands from tiredness.

"Mais alors tu serais libre. Et tu pourrais aller où tu veux. En Angleterre, en Inde... en Provence."

---

[321] perdre la tête – to lose one's mind
[322] démissioner – to resign

My heart begins to pound. I know exactly what she is getting at, but I act innocent:

"Tu veux te débarrasser de moi?" I ask.

"Bien sûr que non. Mais... Lily. *Il te manque.* Je le vois bien."

I close the laptop and stand up.

"Et alors? Il est trop tard. Il est parti en Provence."

"Parle-lui au moins."

"Non."

"Pourquoi es-tu si **têtue**[323]?"

"Qu'est-ce que je dois faire? Est-ce que je dois le **suivre**[324]? Ici, je peux être moi-même. Libre et **indépendante**[325]."

"Lily, tu es une femme créative et intelligente. Réfléchis donc un peu. Ne crois-tu pas que tu

---

[323] têtu – stubborn, pig-headed
[324] suivre – to follow
[325] indépendante – independent

puisses aussi être amoureuse, libre et indépendante?"

"Hmm... je ne sais pas. Je crois que je vais **aller me coucher**[326]. Merci pour ton aide, Claire! Bonne nuit, dors bien!"

---

[326] aller se coucher – to go to bed

# Chapter 14

The following day, I was so tired that I poured myself a large cup of coffee when I arrived at the office at Celuxe. I immediately drop it because of my lack of concentration.

"**Merde**[327]!" I curse loudly, but luckily, no one is there. I try to clean up the mess with a rag, but I cut myself on a piece of porcelain and curse again. It doesn't help. I have to go to the storeroom to get the proper cleaning stuff. I have been avoiding this place - rightly so. When I open the door, I am hit not only by the smell of the old cleaning products but also by the smell of memories. I can no longer fight it. With my bleeding hand, I sit down in the dark room and pull the door shut behind me. The tears come fast and hot. I miss Jacques so much at this moment that it physically hurts. I've done

---

[327] merde - shit

everything I can not to let any feelings in, but it hasn't worked. Eventually, someone opens the door and finds me. Luckily, it is Alika who takes me into her big, soft arms without asking any questions.

Afterwards, I feel like a new person. And I know exactly what I have to do.

With long strides, I storm into Monsieur Dupont's office. It's now or never. He looks at me in surprise.

"Je démissionne!" I call out before I can change my mind.

"Lily, asseyez-vous d'abord," he says with his smugly devilish smile. For a moment, my knees tremble again as I look into his ice-blue eyes.

"Non, je ne m'assieds pas! Je suis ici pour être **franche**[328]."

---

[328] franche – frank, honest

"Vous vous **ridiculisez**[329]."

Oops. I hesitate for a moment. What if he is right? What if I really am making a fool of myself?

"Non. Et je veux vous dire autre chose: vous êtes le **pire**[330] patron que je n'ai jamais eu et ce sera le plus grand plaisir de ne plus jamais avoir à travailler pour quelqu'un comme vous."

"Vous **exagérez**[331]. Vous devez simplement vous **endurcir**[332]. Personne parmi vos collègues ne se plaint non plus."

Again, I am unsettled. Am I exaggerating? Am I just too sensitive? And what if I regret this? What if self-employment doesn't work out after all? Then I can't go back. Shouldn't I keep a little

---

[329] se ridiculiser – to make a fool of oneself
[330] pire (Superlativ von mauvais) – worse
[331] exagérer – to exaggerate
[332] endurcir – to toughen up, grow a thicker skin

194

window open? I breathe in and out deeply. Then I make a decision.

"Je suis sérieuse. Je ne veux plus travailler pour vous ni pour Celuxe."

Monsieur Dupont looks at me. I withstand his gaze, even though it takes all my energy. Finally, he looks away.

"Ok."

"D'accord?"

"J'accepte votre **démission**[333]. C'est bien sûr dommage pour Celuxe de vous perdre. Mais je pense qu'il est préférable pour quelqu'un de votre talent de monter son **propre**[334] business."

"Mais je pensais que vous ne m'aviez promue uniquement parce que Jacques vous l'avait dit..."

---

[333] démission – resignation
[334] propre – own, clean

"Mon fils? Non, il n'a rien à voir avec ça. Les décisions ici, c'est toujours moi qui les prends. En fait, notre relation n'est pas la plus facile depuis que j'ai une nouvelle femme. D'ailleurs, le tableau que vous avez conçu pour ma femme m'a aidé. Merci beaucoup pour cela."

He stands up and shakes my hand.

"Prends soin de toi, Lily."

Why is he so normal all of a sudden? Nice even?

I walk carefully to the door.

"Ah, et Lily?"
"Oui?"
"Dommage que ça n'ait pas marché avec mon fils. J'aurais aimé que vous soyez ma **belle-fille**[335]."

---

[335] belle-fille – daughter-in-law

I am completely perplexed. Had he really just said that? I try to say goodbye politely and leave his office.

As I went home that day with a new sense of freedom, I realised one thing: the 'never fuck the company' was just my protective cloak. I was actually just afraid. I was afraid of not being seen for who I was. Because it happened to me once before, and it hurt me. Yet the saying doesn't matter at all. I am free. It doesn't matter if I work for one company or the other. If working for one company or another doesn't feel good, I don't have to stay. I am not the company. I am a free person, and I can live my life the way I dream. I'm living my life and have the 'only' responsibility of keeping myself happy. No boss, no colleagues, no societal expectations on the CV.

Despite the realisation, I have a sinking feeling in my stomach. I still have the biggest challenge ahead of me: I have to talk to Jacques. I put it off for a long time because I know I have made a mistake. But that doesn't make the situation any better. I have to take action and bear the consequences. So I send him a short message.

"Aurais-tu le temps de parler **prochainement**[336]? J'ai quelque chose à te dire."

---

[336] prochainement   soon

# Chapter 15

He replies instantly, and we arrange to meet tonight. I am relieved that he still wants to see me. The way I treated him was not very nice. It has been weeks since I last saw him. Excited, I take a bath and put on my make-up with extra care. I didn't say anything to my flatmates for the first time, so they didn't make me even more nervous. Finally, the time has come.

I see his picture on the laptop, and the longing for him almost eats me up inside.

"Bonjour Lily... tout va bien?" he asks, and I smile at the sound of his voice. He has cut his hair, but otherwise, he looks as handsome as ever.

"Je vais bien... J'ai démissionné aujourd'hui," I say.

"Oh, wow! **Félicitations**[337]!"

"Merci. Je suis maintenant en freelance. Officiellement."

"C'est génial! Je suis content pour toi!"

"Merci. Comment vas-tu?"

"Il se passe beaucoup de choses de mon coté. Je viens de trouver un nouvel appartement et j'ai quelques nouveaux projets de **peinture**[338] en cours..."

"Alors tu restes en Provence?"

"Oui, pour l'instant je reste..."

"Pourquoi es-tu parti si vite?"

"Je crois que tu sais pourquoi."

And that's when everything bursts out of me:

"Jacques, je suis désolé. Tu **avais raison**[339]. Bien sûr qu'il y avait des sentiments entre nous. Ils étaient là dès le début. Mais je ne voulais pas

---

[337] Félicitation! – Congratulations!
[338] peinture – painting
[339] avoir raison – to be right

200

m'y **engager**[340] parce que... parce que j'avais **peur**[341]."

I sobbed...

"C'est bon."

"Non, ce n'est pas bon! Je n'ai pas été juste. Je n'ai d'abord pas voulu entendre ce que tu voulais me dire, puis je te l'ai reproché. Et je t'ai tout simplement **claqué la porte au nez**[342]! Je suis vraiment désolée pour ça."

"Oui, tu l'as fait," he says, stifling a grin.

"Tu as été une vraie Dupont."

"Maintenant, tu vas trop loin!" I tease him a little before my guilty conscience catches up with me again.

---

[340] engager – to engage, commit, employ
[341] peur – fear
[342] claquer la porte au nez – to slam the door in someone's face

"Honnêtement, je me sens **coupable**[343]. Je suis **incroyablement**[344] désolée de la **façon**[345] dont je t'ai traité. J'ai été **lâche**[346]."

"Ah toi... j'aimerais bien te serrer dans mes bras maintenant," Jacques says and smiles at me lovingly.

"Oui, j'aimerais aussi," I say with a sniffle and blow my nose.

"Pourquoi tu ne viens pas ici?"

I laugh.

"À Nice?"

"Oui, tu es libre maintenant. Tu peux travailler où tu veux. Et j'ai deux amies qui cherchent actuellement une nouvelle colocataire. En y

---

[343] coupble – guilty
[344] incroyablement – incredibly
[345] façon – way, manner
[346] lâche – cowardly

réfléchissant, elles ne sont pas sans ressembler à Claire et Poppy."

"Tu es fou," I say.

"Tu le sais bien."

By the end of the evening, I have a one-way ticket to Nice, two new flatmates, and a monthly pass to a yoga studio in France. I can't believe it, and I could burst with anticipation. I'm going to see Jacques again. This time, not as a 'friend with benefits' but as my boyfriend. I am so excited.

At 5 am, Jacques and I are hanging wearily in front of our screens when he suggests whilst yawning:

"Allons nous coucher, d'accord?"
"Oui! Moi aussi, je suis **fatiguée**[347]."

---

[347] fatiguée – tired

"Et ne t'inquiète pas, je serai parti avant que tu ne te réveilles," Jacques says with a laugh.

"Non, s'il te plaît, ne fais pas ça. Reste, s'il te plaît. Je veux que tu sois là quand je me réveillerai. Ce serait super," I beg him, breaking with my dating constants, and we fall asleep together a little later, and even though it's unusual for our first night together, it's wonderful.

"Surprise!"

For once, I was expecting the third surprise party I've had in the space of a very turbulent year. Tomorrow, my flight leaves for Nice, and Poppy and Claire were all too obvious with their suggestion that I take one last walk around the city to say a proper goodbye. But the walk did me good and reminded me of all the things that have happened here in the course of a year: the affairs and adventures, the many times spent dancing the night away, the professional challenges that ended, not least in a confrontation with the most unpleasant boss in the world and my self-employment. And, of course, the thing with Jacques:

I didn't know how hard it would be for me to admit to falling in love again.

The whole gang is there: Claire and Poppy have decorated the kitchen and invited all my work colleagues and friends: Alika, Vincent, Mailin, Thibault (who grins and beams like it's his party), and even Sarah is there, smiling sheepishly at me. And so we celebrate together one last time.

"Un **discours**[348]!" Poppy shouts, forcing me to stand on the table at a late hour and pull a few words out of my hat.

"Chers amis! Merci d'avoir rendu cette année si **passionnante**[349] pour moi. Je vous suis

---

[348] discours – speech, address, discourse
[349] passionant – passionate

**reconnaissante**[350] pour tout ce qui s'est passé. Le bon et le mauvais. Je sais maintenant que je suis la seule à pouvoir **faire en sorte**[351] d'être heureuse. Je sais que je dois changer ce qui ne me plaît pas et que je dois m'engager pour ce que je souhaite dans ma vie. Je sais que cela en **vaut la peine**[352]. Alors je le fais - je m'envole pour la Provence et je commence mon prochain chapitre avec un homme qui **s'est attaché à mon cœur**[353] cette année. À l'aventure de la vie!"

---

[350] être reconaissant – to be grateful

[351] faire en sorte – to make sure

[352] valoir la peine – to be worth it

[353] s'attacher à son cœur – to capture the heart

# Vocabulary summary

Below, you will find an overview of all translated words in the same order as the vocabulary in the text.

The overview has been compiled with the utmost care. However, no guarantee is given for the accuracy of the content.

1. travail – job, workplace
2. entreprise – company, business
3. graphiste – graphic designer
4. trouver – to find
5. tellement – really, truly
6. beau – beautiful
7. printemps – spring
8. se montre sous son meilleur jour – to show oneself from one's best side
9. nettoyer – to clean
10. colocataire – flatmate
11. au fait – by the way, actually
12. quoique – although
13. se lever – to get up
14. en alternant – alternately
15. pâtisserie – bakery, pastry shop

16. ressembler à qn.– to resemble someone
17. indispensable – essential
18. à quel point – how much
19. jusqu'à présent – up until now
20. à part – apart from
21. brune – brown-haired
22. embêter quelqu'un – to annoy someone
23. gâcher – to spoil, to mess up
24. mignon – cute
25. épouser – to marry
26. se réveiller – to wake up
27. même – even,the same
28. bien qu'elle fasse l'éloge de la virginité tous les dimanches à l'église – even though she praises virginity every Sunday in church
29. le connard – idiot, jerk
30. se défouler – to let off steam
31. coups d'un soir – one-night stand
32. envisager – to consider
33. inspirer – to breathe in
34. détendre – to relax, to loosen
35. accueillir – to welcome
36. cesser – to stop, to cease
37. agrandir – to enlarge, to expand
38. être né(e) – to be born
39. de tous horizons – from all directions, from all over the world
40. le sein maternel – the maternal breast
41. nourrir – to feed, to nourish
42. patron – boss, employer
43. davantage – much more

44. PDG – CEO, managing director
45. souvent – often
46. être occupé – to be busy
47. rare – rare, occasional
48. étroitement – closely
49. main – hand
50. code de conduite – code of conduct
51. à ce sujet – regarding this
52. performant – efficient, high-performing
53. sentir bien – to feel good
54. essayer – to try
55. traiter – to treat
56. amitié – friendship
57. distrayant – distracting
58. en retard – late
59. sauf – except, apart from
60. attendre – to wait, to expect
61. désolé – sorry
62. superbe tenue – stylish outfit
63. avoir envie de – to feel like, to want
64. l'apéro – a pre-meal drink with friends (typically french)
65. boulot – work, job (informal)
66. enchanté(e) (… de faire votre connaissance) – Pleased (… to meet you)!
67. hier – yesterday
68. malheureusement – unfortunately
69. jamais – never
70. travailler à mon compte – to be self employed

71. en tant que nomade numérique – as a digital nomad
72. lieu – place
73. plaire à qn – to appeal to someone
74. postuler – to apply for
75. perdre la tête – to lose one's mind
76. maternelle – nursery
77. dur – hard
78. sale type – nasty guy
79. rejoindre – to meet
80. reconnaissante – grateful
81. rencontrer – to encounter
82. tombé dessus – stumble upon
83. j'avais besoin de changer d'air – I needed a change of scenery
84. séparation – separation
85. baiser – to shag (informal)
86. célibataire – single
87. enfance – childhood
88. Inde – India
89. foule – crowd
90. bonne bouffe – good food (informal)
91. en cachette – in secret
92. se bécoter – to snog
93. sentiments – feelings
94. rester – to stay, to remain
95. scintillante – sparkling
96. se brosser les dents – to brush one's teeth
97. ma chérie – my darling
98. dehors! – Out!
99. association de sans-abri – homeless association

100. tu as une mine affreuse – you look terrible
101. crier – to scream, to shout
102. peur – fear
103. bleu glacé – ice blue
104. haut – tall, high
105. il m'a mis à la porte – he kicked me out
106. craquer quelque chose – to crack something
107. code d'accès – access code
108. domicile nocture – night shelter
109. la boîte – club, box (informal)
110. être encore éveillé – to still be awake
111. morte – dead
112. amener – to bring
113. bonne humeur – good mood
114. Qu'est-ce qui ne va pas chez toi? – What's wrong with you? What is the matter with you? What is going on with you?
115. prévoir – to plan
116. sobre – modest, sober, simple
117. à l'arrière plan – in the background
118. rédiger – to write
119. dessin – drawing
120. l'affiche – poster
121. avoir lieu – to take plce, to occur
122. droit – rights (here: image rights)
123. jet – draft
124. imprimer – to print
125. en colère – angry, furious
126. obtenir – to obtain, to receive
127. grave - serious

128. se défouler sur qn. – to take it out on someone
129. plutôt – rather, instead
130. pourtant – however, yet
131. être horrifié(e) – to be horrified
132. déshériter – to disinherit
133. détendre – to relax, to loosen
134. se lancer – to throw oneself into something
135. tableau – painting
136. cadeau – gift
137. tomber amoureux – to fall in love
138. franchement – frankly
139. énervant(e) – annoying
140. remarquer – to notice
141. empêcher – to prevent
142. mettre à son compte – to go freelance
143. veuillez agréer l'expression de mes salutations distinguées – Yours sincerely
144. briser le cœur – to break the heart
145. vraiment – really
146. droits d'auteur – copyright
147. aucun argent – no money
148. il faut – one must
149. à quoi elle ressemble – what she looks like
150. découvrir – to discover
151. passer inaperçu(e) – to go unnoticed
152. ça fait une éternié – what she looks like
153. chouette – cool, great, a treasure (informal)
154. là-dedans – in there

155. fatigant – tiring, exhausting
156. au-dessus des toilettes – above the toilet
157. affair – business
158. quartier – neighbourhood
159. gars – guy (informal)
160. valeur – value
161. ça ne te regarde pas – it's none of your business
162. réussi(e) – successful
163. souhaiter – to wish
164. entrer quelque part – to go in somewhere
165. se remettre au travail – to get back to work
166. sensé – sensible
167. bouche – mouth
168. remercier – to thank someone
169. aide – help
170. se méprendre – to be mistaken
171. obscures – dark
172. plutôt – rather
173. chaud – hot
174. plaire à quelqu'un – to please someone
175. début – beginning, start
176. éviter – to avoid
177. plage – beach
178. s'améliorer – to improve
179. promettre – to promise
180. devenir meilleur – to get better
181. pleurer – to cry
182. chagrin d'amour – heartbreak
183. à la tienne – cheers (when toasting)
184. paraitre – to seem

185. antipathique – unlikeable
186. mettre mal à l'aise – to make someone feel uncomfortable
187. je te crois sur parole – I take you at your word
188. couper – to cut
189. oreille – ear
190. avoir de la chance – to be lucky
191. gagnant(e) – winner
192. une tournée de boissons – a round of drinks
193. être de la drague – to be a pickup line
194. débarras – storage room
195. harceler – to harass
196. de travers – wrong, askew
197. confus – confused
198. C'est de ma faute. – It's my fault.
199. ne t'en mêle pas! – Don't get involved!
200. zut – damn (informal)
201. régler – to sort out
202. voyage d'affaires – business trip
203. reprendre – to resume
204. endroit – place
205. attraper – to catch, trap, or hold back
206. draguer – to flirt
207. d'abord – first
208. ensuite – then, afterwards
209. d'une certaine manière – in a way
210. profiter de la vie – to enjoy life
211. punition de Dieu – God's punishment
212. faire de mal – to hurt someone

213. culpabiliser – to make someone feel guilty, to feel guilty
214. sage – wise
215. quitter – to leave
216. valise – suitcase
217. concevoir – to design, conceive
218. montre – to show, demonstrate
219. perdre – to lose, waste
220. vite – quickly
221. se mettre à son compte – to start one's own business
222. connards – bastards
223. de toute façon – in any case
224. client – customer, client
225. site internet – website
226. darte de visite – business card
227. connard de patron – bastard boss
228. emploi – employment, job
229. effectivement – indeed, really
230. sembler – to seem, look
231. ennuyeux – boring
232. détester – to hate
233. insolent – cheeky
234. bon sang – oh dear (expression)
235. garder – to keep, store
236. s'assoir – to sit down
237. rendre plus compliqué – to make things more complicated
238. liberté – freedom
239. emménager – to move in
240. paix – peace
241. gentil – nice, kind

242. au moins – at least
243. exciter – to turn on, excite
244. sourcil – eyebrow
245. éternellement – eternally
246. avenir – future
247. réserver – to set aside, reserve
248. plan quinquenal – five-year plan
249. suffire – to be enough
250. bouger – to move
251. endormir – to fall asleep
252. petit déjeuner – breakfast
253. dégoûtant – disgusting
254. convenir – to suit, agree with someone
255. souvenir – to remember
256. dommage – pity
257. fou – crazy
258. fermer – to close
259. clé – key
260. excitant – exciting
261. Chut – shush
262. aspirateur – vacuum cleaner
263. tomber – to fall
264. tout à fait – completely, totally
265. interdire – to forbid
266. en échange – in return
267. inquiéter – to worry someone
268. toute l'équipe – the whole team
269. emmener – to take along
270. tombe – grave
271. promouvoir – to promote
272. poste de direction – managerial position
273. étroitement – closcly

274. service du personnel – human resources department
275. arrêter – to stop
276. cas – case
277. moyen – means, way, method
278. copain – boyfriend
279. mignon – cute, pretty, lovely
280. avouer – to confess, admit
281. truc – thing, stuff
282. au contraire – on the contrary
283. à voir avec le fait – to have to do with the fact
284. pas du tout – not at all
285. découvrir – to discover
286. toxique – toxic
287. stupide – stupid
288. rapport – connection
289. haïr – to hate
290. racontre – to tell
291. lit – bed
292. mettre son grain de sel – to interfere, stick one's oar in
293. convaincre – to convince
294. trop fière – too proud
295. doué – to be gifted
296. défendre – to defend
297. La ferme! – Shut up!
298. bavarder – to chat, gossip
299. rire – to laugh
300. peindre – to paint
301. le marché entre nous – the agreement between us

302. terminer – to finish
303. se manquer – to miss
304. tous les quatre matins – all the time (expression)
305. déménager – to move house
306. Mexique – Mexico
307. sonner – to ring
308. minuit – midnight
309. dehors – outside
310. égal – equal, indifferent
311. s'enfuir – to escape
312. au juste – actually
313. recommencer – to start again
314. triste – sad
315. lien – link, connection
316. mériter – to deserve
317. côté – side
318. punir qqn./qqch. – to punish someone for something
319. faire diversion – to divert attention
320. C'est le ciel qui vous envoie! – You're heven-sent! (expression)
321. perdre la tête – to lose one's mind
322. démissioner – to resign
323. têtu – stubborn, pig-headed
324. suivre – to follow
325. indépendante – independent
326. aller se coucher – to go to bed
327. merde - shit
328. franche – frank, honest
329. se ridiculiser – to make a fool of oneself
330. pire (Superlativ von mauvais) – worse

331. exagérer – to exaggerate
332. endurcir – to toughen up, grow a thicker skin
333. démission – resignation
334. propre – own, clean
335. belle-fille – daughter-in-law
336. prochainement – soon
337. Félicitation! – Congratulations!
338. peinture – painting
339. avoir raison – to be right
340. engager – to engage, commit, employ
341. peur – fear
342. claquer la porte au nez – to slam the door in someone's face
343. coupble – guilty
344. incroyablement – incredibly
345. façon – way, manner
346. lâche – cowardly
347. fatiguée – tired
348. discours – speech, address, discourse
349. passionant – passionate
350. être reconaissant – to be grateful
351. faire en sorte – to make sure
352. valoir la peine – to be worth it
353. s'attacher à son cœur – to capture the heart

# Epilogue

Dear reader,

You've reached the end of this bilingual romance novel – thank you so much for coming along on Lily's journey!

Did you enjoy the story? Did you find the language experience helpful?

I'd love to hear your thoughts – either as a short review on Amazon or via a personal message on my website:
www.bilingual-novels.com.

Would you like to read more bilingual love stories in the future?

Then here's an idea: **join my test reader community** and read the next books **for free** – before they're officially published!

Simply sign up on my website, and you'll be among the first to hear when a new title is ready to explore.

*P.S.: No worries about email overload – I usually take a few months to write and polish each book (in two languages!).*

Thank you again for reading – and I hope we'll meet again on the pages of another bilingual adventure.

All the best,
Lucy Lagarde

223

Printed in Dunstable, United Kingdom